The liberal person shall be enriched."

Prov. 11:25 NIV

Also by

Kevin Gerald

Characteristics of a Winner
Developing Confidence
Habits/Overcoming Negative Behavior
The Proving Ground
Raising Champion Children

PARDON ME,
I'M
PROSPERING

PARDON ME,
I'M PROSPERING

KEVIN GERALD

Kevin Gerald Communications ● Tacoma, Washington

Published by Kevin Gerald Communications
1819 East 72nd Street
Tacoma WA 98404

First Edition 1998

ISBN: 0-9661247-4-X

Manufactured in the United States of America
Tacoma WA

10 9 8 7 6 5 4 3 2 1

CONTENTS

No one would remember the good Samaritan if he only had good intentions. He had money as well.
— Margaret Thatcher

INTRODUCTION

Bill Gates, the world's wealthiest individual, was recently hit in the face with pies by two strangers. This was shortly after he had received a threatening letter from a man who ordered him to pay five million dollars or die. Although these are extreme reactions, it is not unusual for prosperous people to experience negative attitudes and behavior from people around them. Unfortunately, the church is not exempt from this resentment against those who prosper.

This book is written *on behalf of every Christian who has felt as if they must apologize for experiencing prosperity in their life.* The over emphasis on the dangers of pursuing worldly gain has left many Christians feeling condemned to a lifetime of lack and insufficiency. In recent generations, one of the markings of a man or woman of God could be determined by their willingness to own little or nothing of this world's goods. Unfortunately, many talented and gifted people were *not* taught that they could "serve God and have money." Instead, they were taught that they couldn't "serve God and serve money." This slight variation of truth and lack of accurate understanding has been damaging. It forced many to either *condemn* themselves out of relationship with God or deny their God-given power to get wealth.

WEALTH TO US IS NOT
MERE MATERIAL FOR
VAIN-GLORY BUT AN
OPPORTUNITY FOR
ACHIEVEMENT. POVERTY
WE THINK IT NO
DISGRACE TO
ACKNOWLEDGE, BUT
A REAL
DEGRADATION TO MAKE
NO EFFORT TO
OVERCOME.
—*THUCYDIDES, 415 BC*

Chapter 1

PROSPERITY IS A BIBLE WORD

A few years ago, I requested that my assistant print out all the Biblical references to prosperity. I remember watching as the computer paper literally piled up on the floor. I then took that pile of scripture references to the platform and rolled it out so the church could see that prosperity is *definitely* a Bible word.

The word *prosper* means "to have continued success, to thrive, to grow, to be flourishing, to have wealth and good fortune." The word *prosper* in its various tenses appears approximately ninety times in the

Bible. A few examples are listed below.

"The Lord was with Joseph and he prospered..."
Genesis 39:2 (NIV)

(referring to Joshua) "That thou mayest prosper
withersoever thou goest."
Joshua 1:7 (KJV)

"Let the Lord be magnified, which hath pleasure in the
prosperity of His servant."
Psalms 35:27 (KJV)

"When the righteous prosper the city rejoices.
Proverbs 11:10 (NIV)

"A generous man will prosper."
Proverbs 11:25 (NIV)

" ...he who trusts in the Lord will prosper."
Proverbs 28:25 (NIV)

" For I know the plans I have for you,' declares
the Lord, 'plans to prosper you'..."
Jeremiah 29:11 (NIV)

"He will make you more prosperous..."
Deuteronomy 30:5 (NIV)

"The Lord will again delight in you and make you prosperous." **Deuteronomy 30:9 (NIV)**

"Whatever he does (the Godly man) prospers." **Psalms 1:3 (NIV)**

"He will spend his days in prosperity..." **Psalms 25:13 (NIV)**

To hear some Christians comment on prosperity you would think that prosperity, or the desire to prosper, is an evil, sinful desire. For a long time, many within church circles have held the notion that prosperity is evidence of being unspiritual. Beliefs such as "Jesus had nowhere to lay His head", or "He used a borrowed donkey," have been used as arguments against prosperity. According to this school of thinking, Christians should not live in plenty but "just get by." In contrast, *the Bible describes prosperity as something that happens when we walk in the principles of God's word.*

Even today some Christians feel guilty when they prosper. This often stems from wrong teaching by many that equate prosperity with being ungodly, and poverty with being spiritual! Recently, while being interviewed by a local newspaper reporter, I was asked why I drive a nice car. The reporter pointed out that,

15

as a sign of their devotion to God, ministers are not supposed to have nice things. I quickly responded that being a Christian or a minister did not mean that I have taken a "vow of poverty." This surprised him because he had assumed, based on the traditional religious mind-set, that poverty vows were a prerequisite to being in ministry. Unfortunately, this is the assumption most people have, not only about ministers, but about anyone they would refer to as a "religious" person.

This inaccurate assumption has even caused countless numbers of people who believe in God to conclude that there is a conflict with their desire to be devoted Christians and their desire to prosper. An example of this is in the book *God and Mammon in America* by Robert Wuthnaw.

Warren Means attended Catholic elementary and secondary schools, graduated from college in economics, and served four years in the air force. By age twenty-eight, he worked his way up to controller of a small aeronautics firm but then decided it was time to move on. After two years earning an MBA at Harvard, he took a position at one of the nation's largest banks, eventually enlarging his responsibilities until he had oversight of approximately $1.2 billion in loans. Then, realizing he had risen as far as he could, he quit and with a few other investors bought a small air transport business that *specializes in international freight. Ten years later, following some internal financial structuring that left him a wealthy man, Means has built the firm into an operation that handles about $40 million in sales annually.*

It's been a long time since he's been to church, although he still considers himself a Catholic. He's been busy. But he's also a bit miffed at the church. It taught him that money was the root of all evil and to think badly of the money changers in the temple. He was never quite able to reconcile those views with being a banker. "I guess I must have been a very bad person!" He figures the best way to reconcile religion and the material world is by keeping them apart. "Money," he says, "is a technical matter. If you tried to follow the Bible, you'd never get anywhere!"

Unfortunately, this is the widespread conclusion of many people today. They have bought into the thinking that began in medieval times when church leaders believed that merchandising and the accumulation of goods was not only an antisocial behavior, but also a sign of a corrupt soul. Although this thinking is being challenged by more and more people who are studying the Bible, most of society has not yet corrected inaccurate beliefs and assumptions that are hundreds of years old. Mother Teresa was an example of what society assumes all devoted Christians should be. While I admire Mother Teresa's tenacious efforts on behalf of the poor, everyone is not called to those same lifetime efforts. *In fact, you would be hard pressed to find biblical heroes who spent their lifetime feeding and clothing the impoverished.* The Bible characters that are most often written about were people who were devoted to God and expressed their devotion through:

* Accumulation of land and livestock.
* The building and rebuilding of cities and nations.
* Increase in silver, gold, and valued stones.
* Rising to positions of influence in society.
* Promoting and legislating godliness in the land.

It's certainly not my intention to discredit the outstanding and diligent efforts of Mother Teresa. However, as I listened to the news commentators reporting on her death and funeral, it was obvious that much of the world still thinks that her life and works are the *only* picture of a deeply devoted *religious* person.

When the lies were born, I'm not sure. However, in the early sixteenth century, the church had greater wealth than the state. Perhaps a combination of mismanagement by church officials and a desire of the state to take over, created a climate for the message of "poor is better." This message has weakened the church's ability to lead and influence society. If the people who are God-conscious are reduced to a life of insufficiency and lack, then who will promote and support the things we believe in: The Hollywood stars? The Rock-n-Roll stars? The government? Is it any wonder that universities like Harvard and Oxford began as Christian institutions and eventually were attended and administrated by non-Christians? Christian youth were getting the message that "good Christians" don't pursue education and careers. Is it any surprise that very few Christians of our generation have experienced wealth and prosperity?

Most of the myths about money that some Christians have accepted as truth do have their origin in scripture. They are, however, a result of wrong conclusions about the meaning of scripture. The topic of prosperity and blessing upon the righteous is a theme of the Bible. It is like a continued thread weaving its way through the Old and New Testaments alike. The anti-prosperity teaching isolates a small number of scriptures and represents them as the main scriptures, rather than the balancing scriptures. Anytime you access something of power, it always comes with warning labels. These labels are not intended to tell you that you should not have the microwave oven or the lawn mower, but rather to guide and instruct you in their proper use. The Bible approaches the accumulation of wealth in the same way. It warns us about the dangers of this powerful instrument if it is misused or abused. But at the same time, it encourages us to prosper and promises God's abundant provision and increase to those who believe and receive it.

CHALLENGING THE BELIEFS THAT HINDER PROSPERITY. The reason some Christians don't prosper is not because God doesn't want them to prosper, but because they have beliefs that hinder them from prospering. Wrong beliefs lead to wrong actions. This is why Jesus said, "According to your faith... so be it unto you." (Matthew 9:29.) This is the law of faith, and it's at work in our lives whether we realize it or not. *Our believing affects our receiving.* For hundreds of years the "flat-world theory" hindered exploration. Men dared not to venture far from their home because of the belief they would fall off the edge of the earth. What were they missing out on? Only time would reveal the vast and beautiful world of opportunities that awaited them. The limiting beliefs that hindered exploration were all myths with a widespread acceptance as truth. The peer pressure exerted by sailors created a common acceptance of the flat-world theory. As we know today, the myth was eventually recognized as a wrong, mistaken belief. It was only after the belief was changed that men were able to expand their territory and experience the wealth of new, fertile lands. This book is only one of many being written to challenge the beliefs that hinder God's people from prospering. As we correct our beliefs, our actions and our choices will move us toward vast opportunities of increase.

A BIBLE FRAME OF REFERENCE

There are pictures in all our minds which can be referred to as our frame of reference. In much the same way that a key word can access information in a computer, our minds access our own individual perspective at the very sound of a key word. This perspective is the frame of reference upon which we act, speak, and form opinions. Before some people can experience prosperity they must first change their frame of reference about prosperity. These individuals have negative assumptions about prosperity that will cause them to repel prosperity throughout their life. Rather than experiencing prosperity, these people have a history of bad breaks and missed opportunities. Our frame of reference forms through personal experiences and concepts passed on to us by those around us. God's word is the answer to a wrong frame of reference about prosperity.

For example, the person who associates prosperity with gangsters, swindlers, and con-artists needs a new and revised frame of reference about prosperity. This person should meditate on God's word which declares:

"A generous man will prosper."
Proverbs 11:25 (NIV)

"Prosperity is the reward of the righteous."
Proverbs 13:21 (NIV)

"Whoever gives heed to instruction prospers."
Proverbs 16:20 (NIV)

"He who trusts in the Lord will prosper."
Proverbs 28:25 (NIV)

Another kind of person who needs a new frame of reference is the person who feels destined for a "barely-get-by" life and future. Most people who have this mind-set about life think it's just common sense. They often work hard and live frugally. If you listen to them talk, they consistently refer to money as if there is little to go around. Although these people do not usually get into excessive debt or suffer financial devastation, neither do they experience their prosperity potential. Their lives are often lived in fear and worry due to the mind-set of insufficiency. This person should meditate on God's word which declares:

"...You will be prosperous and successful."
Joshua 1:8 (NIV)

"The Lord will grant you abundant prosperity."
Deuteronomy 28:11 (NIV)

"You will always be at the top, never at the bottom."
Deuteronomy 28:13 (NIV)

"...Your God will make you most prosperous..."
Deuteronomy 30:9 (NIV)

"You will be made rich in every way..."
II Corinthians 9:11 (NIV)

FRUITFUL, ENDURING AND PROSPEROUS

In Psalm One we have a powerful word picture of a prosperous person. The descriptive nature of this writing clarifies what we can expect when our thinking is molded by the word of God. When you read this, notice the emphasis to avoid ungodly counsel and the influence of people who are in error. A lot of good people have been affected by wrong thinking and inaccurate perceptions about prosperity. If you allow others, whoever they may be, to shape your thoughts contrary to God's thoughts, you hinder His work of prosperity in your life. The people around us often mean well, but are in serious contradiction to God's perspective. The second thing I want you to notice when you read this Psalm is that the man who delights in, and meditates on God's word is fruitful, enduring, and prosperous. Now read it and see the picture, the frame of reference.

"Blessed is the man who does not walk in the counsel of the wicked or stand in the way of sinners or sit in the seat of mockers. But his delight is in the law of the Lord and on His law he meditates day and night. He is like a tree planted by streams of water, which yields its fruit in season and whose leaf does not wither. Whatever he does prospers."
Psalm 1:1-3 (NIV)

Can you take this picture and use it to replace all the questions concerning God's intentions for your life? Why not put this reference deep within yourself as the target for your future?

If this proclamation of a Godly person is important enough that it was God-breathed into scripture, why not personalize it as a proclamation over your life? How would this frame of reference affect your life if you were to say every day, "I delight and meditate in God's word, therefore I am like a tree which is fruitful, enduring and everything I do prospers."

*"THE LORD WILL
GRANT YOU ABUNDANT
PROSPERITY..."*
DEUTERONOMY 28:11

Chapter 2

FIVE MYTHS ABOUT MONEY

> ## Myth #1
> ## Money is the root of all evil.

A myth is a traditional story of unknown authorship. Among some Christians, the myths about money are usually accepted as truth because they are widespread and span several generations of time and tradition.

The scripture origin of this myth reads like this:

"For the love *of money is the root of all kinds of evil."*
I Timothy 6:10 (NIV)

Notice first that the scripture is not addressing money, but rather the *"love of money."* We see this in society today. People do evil things when they "love" money.

- People embezzle funds from their own employer, the person who hired and trusted them, when they love money.
- People neglect their marriage and family relationship, because they love money.
- Sales people and business owners often deceive customers and compromise their own character because they love money.
- People pretend to be in love with a wealthy person and sometimes marry them when in reality they only love their money.
- Spouses murder their mate and make it look like an accident in an attempt to collect money from an insurance company.
- Thiefs and gangs attack people, often harming them, to take their money.
- Brothers and sisters forfeit their relationship, fighting over an inheritance.
- Every day, casino gamblers lose everything they have to support themselves and their children trying to get more money.

These are the kind of evils that the Bible is referencing when it states "the love of money is the root of all evil."

When my wife Sheila and I built our first home, we were so excited about the neighborhood we were moving into. We had been attracted to the quality which was obvious in the existing homes and future development plans. As we read the homeowner's covenants, it became apparent that we would have to spend some additional money to build a home that would comply with the covenants. Although it cost us extra, we made some changes in the materials used for building and landscaping. The developer insisted we do it, so we agreed, knowing that those quality controls throughout the neighborhood would benefit everyone.

After finishing our home and living in it for a couple of years, we noticed that homes of lesser quality were going in around us. Before long, rumors of lawsuits were echoing down the streets as homeowners saw the value of their homes compromised by less expensive homes. As it turned out, the developer had decided to *not* uphold the covenants since the lots were not selling fast enough. It meant less to him that homeowners were treated fairly and he remain a man of his word, than to make some *faster money*.

Get it straight in your mind that money, in and of itself, is *neither good* nor *evil.* It is like electricity that can heat a home or burn down a home. It has potential to do good or do harm, based on who has it and how they use it. Power is the same. Power can build a nation or corrupt it. It is not in and of itself either evil or good.

So, before continuing to think that money is evil, come a little closer to the meaning of the scripture and discern the message as it's intended. Realize that this myth has caused some people to actually repel money-making opportunities in their life. This myth must be eliminated from your conscious and subconscious mind or it will hinder your prosperity. When a person wholeheartedly believes the truth about money and realizes that money is not evil, they position themselves to *attract*, *increase*, and *experience* prosperity.

Myth #2
A rich person has less chance of salvation than a camel has of squeezing through the eye of a sewing needle.

The scripture that generates this myth is Matthew 19:23, 24 which reads like this:

"And Jesus said to His disciples, Truly I say to you, it will be difficult for a rich man to get into the kingdom of heaven. Again I tell you, it is easier for a camel to go through the eye of a needle than for a rich man to go into the kingdom of heaven." (AMP)

For a better understanding of this scripture, I would encourage you to consider some of the preceding verses. A rich man is put to the test of priorities. Although some readers conclude that Jesus was insisting that he give up all that he had, I find that to be inconsistent with the rest of the Bible. If giving up possessions is a requirement for men to enter the Kingdom of God, then why aren't all the wealthy heroes of scripture commanded to do the same? *This was not an issue of a man having money; this was an issue of money having a man.* I believe that Jesus saw the priority this man placed on his wealth as a hindrance to him in being able to make Christ the Lord of his life Had this man said yes to Jesus' command, instead of walking away sorrowful, he would have inherited the kingdom *and retained his earthly wealth.* How? I believe Jesus would have done what God did after commanding Abraham to give up his son Isaac. He stopped him from doing it as *soon as He knew he was willing.* It was in this setting that Jesus made the comment about the camel and the needle's eye.

> *"When the disciples heard this, they were greatly astonished and asked, "Who then can be saved?"*
> *Matthew 19:25 (NIV)*

This verse indicates that the disciples who themselves had homes, land, servants, and wealth were now saying among themselves, "who then can be saved?" (If riches can keep a person out of the kingdom, where does that leave most of us?) Jesus then comforted them by assuring them that a rich man can, by God's grace in his life, enter the Kingdom of God (verse 26).

> *"Jesus looked at them and said, 'With man this is impossible, but with God all things are possible."*
> *Matthew 19:26 (NIV)*

That assurance is a testimony to the fact that people who answer the call of salvation can make Christ the Lord of their life and still have wealth. Jesus is saying if man were on his own, he would be governed by his own thoughts and concepts of life. But, with God in his life, a proper attitude of wealth, and an acceptance of biblical principles, a rich man will inherit the Kingdom of God. If you're a committed Christian who has a growing business, you should rejoice at this revelation of scripture. Don't feel condemned, but rather be thankful that God sees your commitment to Him. If you accept His lordship, He makes it possible for you to be saved and continue increasing in your life. He makes it possible for you to have money without money having you!

Another interesting possibility referenced in Victor's Handbook of Bible Knowledge (p. 466) is that Jesus was referring to the smaller of two gates in the city walls, which was called the Needle's Eye. It was a gate within the larger gate at the entrance of the city. Although intended for people, a camel could get through the Needle's Eye if it were unloaded and on its knees. Merchants and travelers did not like to do this because it required effort and sacrifice. Sometimes, however, when city gates were closed they were forced to. With this in mind, Jesus could have been saying that rich people must humble themselves and *unload* their wealth to enter the kingdom. In other words, lay it all on the altar before God, give it all up in heartfelt surrender. Only after doing so can a rich person "get in." However, the good news is, as we've seen time and again, God gives it back after we genuinely give it up! So, like the camel getting loaded back up once inside the city, the rich people who enter the kingdom find that God is a God of continued blessing and provision upon His people.

Myth #3
If God wants me to have prosperity, He will give it to me, without me asking for it.

This myth is typically spoken by people who feel uncomfortable asking God to prosper them. Nehemiah, on the other hand, boldly approached God with a request for prosperity.

"O Lord... let now thine ear be attentive to the prayer of thy servant... and prosper, I pray thy servant this day..." Nehemiah 1:11 (KJV)

If the logic was biblical that "whatever God wants us to have He gives us," then why do we only receive salvation by asking? Does God want us to be saved? Absolutely! Does He save us without us asking Him to? Of course not! The same is true for all that God wants to give us.

"Ask and it will be given to you; seek and you will find; knock and the door will be opened to you. For everyone who asks receives; he who seeks finds; and to him who knocks, the door will be opened. "Which of you, if his son asks for bread, will give him a stone? Or if he asks for a fish, will give him a snake? If you, then, though you are evil, know how to give good gifts to

your children, how much more will your Father in
heaven give good gifts to those who ask him! "
Matthew 7:7-11 (NIV)

"Asking" is acknowledging God as our source. It's a compliment to God when a person approaches Him with their needs and desires.

"Therefore I tell you, whatever you ask for in prayer,
believe that you have received it, and it will be yours."
Mark 11: 24 (NIV)

For some people, this third myth is also rooted in the thought that God may not view natural needs as important as those of the inner man. While there is no doubt that God's plan for our lives is a prosperity that works from the inside out, it doesn't mean that He's not interested about our natural, physical, and financial prosperity.

Let them shout for joy, and be glad, that favor my
righteous cause: yea, let them say continually, Let the
Lord be magnified, which hath pleasure
in the prosperity of his servant."
Psalm 35:27 (KJV)

Many people settle for a lot less than God would like to see them have. One writer described this approach to life like this:

I bargained with life for a penny only to find out in dismay, that whatever I had asked of life, life would have paid. — (unknown)

Our expectations have a powerful effect on what we receive in life. As Christians, a wrong belief about God's intentions for our lives creates a self-imposed limitation. The limitation is not with God, it is in us. If you are not currently praying for prosperity, perhaps there is a subtle question in your mind causing you to hesitate. That question is a contradiction to the word of God, and according to II Corinthians 10:5, it should be demolished and brought into obedience to God's word.

On a ministry trip to Asia, my daughter Jodi had requested I try to find her a specific camera. After stopping at four or five shops in Hong Kong, I started to realize it might not be as easy to find as I had assumed. With only one day to find this specific camera, I soon found myself in back streets, front streets, and camera shops of all sizes. I was determined not to go home without the camera my daughter wanted. I was ready to do everything within my power to grant her request. Finally I scored, and the look of joy on her face when I gave it to her made it all worthwhile. In Matthew 7:11, Jesus said that if we know how to give good gifts to our children, how much more will our heavenly father give good gifts to those who ask Him!

Eight Reasons Why God Wants Us To Prosper

1. To establish His covenant in the earth. (Deuteronomy 8:18)
2. Because He delights in the prosperity of His "servant". (Psalms 35:27)
3. So we can leave an inheritance for our children's children. (Proverbs 13:22)
4. So we can live without worry for the things we need. (Matthew 6:25-33)
5. So we can have all sufficiency, in all things and give an abundance to good works. (II Corinthians 9:6-8)
6. To accomplish God's will, which is to transfer wealth from the Kingdom of Darkness to the Kingdom of Light. (Proverbs 13:22)
7. So we can be the "head" and not the "tail;..." lend with no need to borrow. (Deuteronomy 28:12-13)
8. Because we are His children and He wants to give us good things (Matthew 7:11)

Myth #4
Owning possessions = Materialism

Materialism is a word that has been used to discourage Christians from the accumulation of assets. Materialism, however, is not the mere possession of things. Materialism is the undisciplined appetite that causes a person to be governed and controlled by a desire for more. If simply having possessions was wrong, why does the Bible speak so "matter of factly" of the possessions owned by individuals who had God's favor?

SOLOMON
II Chronicles 9:3, 4, 13, 20, 21, 25, 28

The Queen of Sheba was impressed when she came to visit Solomon. She saw his wisdom, the house he had built, the meat on his table (evidently not fast food) as well as his servants and their apparel (even his servants dressed well).

The weight of gold in one year's income for Solomon was twenty-five tons. His throne was ivory, overlaid with pure gold. His drinking glasses were gold. Every three years his ships went to Tarshish to bring back gold, silver, ivory, apes, and peacocks. Solomon had four thousand stalls for horses and chariots. His horses were the finest from Egypt and around the world.

Solomon had all kinds of stuff! He was the rich guy with all the luxuries in his generation. In the minds of many people today, it's not possible for a person to be that wealthy, have that much stuff and be in right standing with God. However, Solomon was not only a righteous man, he was a gifted, Godly leader in his nation who built a tremendous house for the Lord.

ABRAM AND LOT
Genesis 13:2, 5, 6

Abram and Lot were very rich in cattle, silver, gold, flocks, herds, and tents. In fact, they had so much prosperity that they experienced "growing pains." The land they were on could not accommodate their increase of goods. Abraham's servant said that "the Lord had blessed his master with flocks, herds, silver, gold and menservants and maidservants and camels and donkeys." (Genesis 24:35) Imagine, the Lord being declared the provider of Abram's stuff! Oftentimes it is hard for our modern minds to fully appreciate things like camels and donkeys. To actually realize the comparison would be to compare those camels to big eighteen-wheel trucks used for transportation. The donkeys would be comparable to automobiles today. The servants would be like employees on your payroll. Chariots, as in Solomon's situation, would be like a luxury model vehicle... Mercedes, Rolls Royce. In fact, if these Bible characters lived today, they would no doubt have the best in transportation, including airplanes and helicopters.

JOB
Job 42:12

Job had always been a prosperous man, but the Lord blessed Job with twice as much in the later years of his life. He had 14,000 sheep, 6,000 camels, 1,000 yoke of oxen, and 1,000 female donkeys. Often when people who have great wealth enter a season of loss, people speculate that it must be God's judgment on their life-style. Since we have a "behind the scenes" look at Job's life, we know that God did not cause the crisis in Job's life. However, God did use it as a time of pruning for Job that eventually caused him to flourish more than ever before. The key is to never doubt that God's intentions for us are good. Do not allow a temporary setback to be thought of as a permanent condition, but rather as an opportunity for a comeback in our lives. One of God's specific words to His people that He repeated often through prophets in the Old Testament was "I will restore your fortunes." (Deuteronomy 30:3, Jeremiah 30:18, 32:44, 33:11 and 48:47) This isn't a reference to *you* as a spiritual being, but a promise that He will restore your natural and material possessions as well. "The land, the gold, the livestock.... I will restore all of those things." This was a familiar promise from God unto His people.

DAVID
I Chronicles 29:2-5

In our nation today, which is structured as a democratic society, our president has a tremendous amount of resources available to him. The house he lives in, the automobiles and planes he rides in, the dinners he hosts, the phone calls he makes, the retreats he takes are just a sampling of resources he can utilize. In the time of David's kingship, the monarchy was especially structured to give the king liberty with the resources of the kingdom. David utilized this freedom to provide gold, silver, bronze, iron, wood, onyx, stones, marble and all necessary materials and manpower to build the house of God. In addition to that, however, David gave of his personal wealth $87,255,000 in gold and $13,440,000 in silver for a total offering of $100,695,000 to the building of the temple! David's generosity extended beyond allocating national funds toward the temple; he gave of his own personal wealth. It is from his giving that we get an idea of the vastness of his personal riches. Anyone who can give an offering of this size from his personal wealth is a man of astounding financial strength. So why is it that many Christians immediately condemn people as being materialistic if they have more "stuff" than the average person? If these Bible characters were loaded with exorbitant amounts of wealth, and the "stuff" that accompanies wealth, why is it so quickly criticized by believers today? If a person has houses, land, cars, boats and airplanes, does that mean they love God less? Does having material possessions mean a person is "materialistic?"

DIFFERENT IS NOT "BETTER" OR "WORSE"

In my experience as a pastor, I've witnessed greed in various forms. Amazingly, greed presides in no specific economic class, but exists in all levels of society. It also manifests itself in different ways. For example, it is just as common to see a family of average income struggle with greed as it is for a family with a much larger income. Sometimes the driving force of greed is "I fear losing what I have so, I must save, save, save." While other times, the driving force of greed is to satisfy the appetite for more toys, gadgets, clothes, etc. Greed is not always evidenced by life-style. Excessive saving or excessive spending can be indicators of greed. I have Christian friends who prefer to save and make long-term investments while their home is modest. Their car is modest, and their clothes are very inexpensive, and they have few, if any, "toys".

These people have a definite plan for what they want to do with their income, and most of it is based on long-term financial security. I also have Christian friends who save less than this first group of people and choose to live a higher life-style. They choose to spend more to have more space to raise their family, take children on vacations, drive nice automobiles and wear nice clothes. Neither of these lifestyles is necessarily wrong. As long as the conservative person provides well for his family, and is not too tight to make great memories with them. The conservative should always remind himself that today is important too, and that kids only grow up once. He must enjoy the journey. The less conservative person should consider the future, and guard against excessive debt that occurs when trying to live a life-style he can't afford. He should keep in mind the long-term issues such as college funds and retirement, and prepare for them.

If each type of person guards against neglect of the present or the future, neither is wrong. It's just a matter of personal preference.

But what about the fact that Christians who spend on a higher life-style could be giving more to God's kingdom and worthwhile causes? Isn't the choice to spend on their own luxuries an irresponsible choice? When seeking to give a fair and honest response to that question we must consider the following:

1. God doesn't require anywhere that people give more than the tithe and offerings. Unlike the IRS, the Bible does not expect the higher income person to give a higher percentage than the lower income person. The heavy taxation of the rich is an unfair penalization of prosperity. God's requirements are impartial and fair.
2. I personally know higher-income Christians who spend money on luxuries, and also *give* generously to the kingdom. When people question the heart of a person who has luxuries, without knowing their giving habits, it's an unfair and improper conclusion.

In the writings of Paul to the young Pastor Timothy, he gave him some guidance for instructing the rich members of his congregation:

"Command those who are rich in this present world not to be arrogant nor to put their hope in wealth, which is so uncertain, but to put their hope in God, who richly provides us with everything for our enjoyment. Command them to do good, to be rich in good deeds, and to be generous and willing to share."
I Timothy 6:17, 18 (NIV)

Let's review the instructions:

* Don't be arrogant, thinking you are better than others.
* Don't put your hope in wealth, but put your hope in God *who* richly provides everything *for* our enjoyment. See God as the creator of the wealth you enjoy!
* Do good and be rich in good deeds.
* Be generous and willing to share.

Nowhere in this instruction is there any insinuation that the rich Christian should feel condemnation for being rich. Neither does it say "tell them to sell their houses, land, cattle, and luxuries to give to worthwhile causes in the Kingdom of God."

This was definitely Paul's chance to speak clearly on the life-style of the rich. The exhortation was specific but did not condemn them having wealth.

Myth #5
"All Christian leaders want
is my money."

This is one of the most common complaints among those who criticize Bible teaching churches today. The fact is, however, that the subject of money is one of the most common themes in the Bible. The scriptures address financial issues from various perspectives such as:

◆Earning	◆Giving
◆Receiving	◆Saving
◆Tithing	◆Inheritance
◆Sharing	◆Enjoying
◆Investing	◆Sowing and Reaping
◆Planning	◆Spending

Most of society today see a church as a charity organization. The TV personalities, media, and journalists involved with forming public opinion are, for the most part, ignorant of scripture. To complicate matters, today's religious leaders have been afraid to speak freely on the subject of finances, for fear of being criticized or losing church members.

Even though Jesus' teachings are relevant and deal with the issues of life, most schools of theology today steer clear of this direct life-style approach. They prefer to focus on intellectual depths of theology that are of little benefit to man. The result is widespread ignorance on biblical teachings of finances. An additional consequence is a society that assumes this is the way it is supposed to be, and that the Bible is only about peace and love. So, modern man turns on the TV to a tele-evangelist, or attends a Bible teaching church and becomes defensive. Some are convinced that Christian leaders who talk about money are charlatans whose primary interest is to get somebody's money.

Because this scene is so common today, Christian leaders tiptoe around the subject of money not wanting to be misunderstood.

The church has been weakened by its passive position on finances. It's biblical form of support, tithes and offerings, has been undercut to the point where most churches struggle financially. God's financial plan, if taught and obeyed, would cause churches to flourish in their communities. Instead, they have lights burned out, buildings worn out, and insufficient funds. According to James Grant, Executive Director of UNICEF "If church members would tithe...the increase of income in churches would provide enough to eliminate the worst of world poverty (an estimated 65 billion dollars) and still have an additional 17 billion dollars to use in other ways without changing what churches currently receive." Of course, Mr. Grant's primary concern is world relief, and although that's not what tithes are designated for, his figures give us an idea of how much the church could do if every member tithed.

In 1933, during the great depression, church members were giving an estimated 3.3 percent of their income to churches. This figure has been declining ever since, in spite of the fact that our nation is more prosperous than ever.

The only way the attitude towards the church's right to teach and collect finances will change is by a fresh and accurate understanding by both leaders and congregations. An understanding that:

- Church leaders are under obligation to teach Bible economics, including tithes and offerings.
- The strength of the church is directly related to its giving habits.
- Failure to bring tithes and offerings is scripturally considered "robbing" God.
- Tithes and offering are a prerequisite to blessings upon our churches.
- Prayer, testimonies, and programs are not replacements for proper giving.
- If you're a tither, you are in the minority among

church goers. Don't take the continued reference to finances personally. Pray for and encourage your leaders to speak boldly on this subject.

"...THE KINGDOM OF THE WORLD HAS BECOME THE KINGDOM OF OUR LORD ... HE WILL REIGN FOREVER AND EVER."
REVELATION 11:15

Chapter 3

THE DOMINION MANDATE

THE DOMINION MANDATE

> *"God blessed them and said to them,'Be fruitful and increase in number; fill the earth and subdue it. Rule over the fish of the sea and the birds of the air and over every living creature that moves on the ground.' "*
> *Genesis 1:28 (NIV)*

In the above scripture, God instructs man to rule over the earth. Notice what He says. "Fill the earth, subdue it and rule over everything in it." This mandate from

God describes man's rightful position and proper approach to life on earth. The idea that many Christians have about "this ol' world" is that we should just get through it as best we can. They renounce its value assuming it's worthless to God and unworthy of their time and attention. This is a violation of the dominion mandate. In fact, before we can legitimately rule over spiritual things, we should be capable of ruling over natural things (cattle, fish, birds). *Some people are trying to take authority over principalities and powers in the heavenlies and they can't even clean their garages*! Some people are trying to rule over devils, but have no control over their own tongue. Jesus said, "... whatever you bind on earth will be bound in heaven,..." (Matthew 16:19) Notice the sequence is "earthly" or natural things are bound *first*, then "heavenly" or spiritual things are bound. Jesus also taught that the way we handle financial matters may qualify us to be trustworthy with true riches.

"So if you have not been trustworthy in handling worldly wealth, who will trust you with true riches?"
Luke 16:11 (NIV)

People who overlook the importance of ruling over the natural will eventually be brought down and overcome by natural forces. *I've seen Christians whose lives are literally devastated and their faith shipwrecked, because they underestimated the importance of taking dominion in the natural, physical world.* They were doing the right things spiritually, but neglecting their responsibility of rulership over earthly things. The dominion mandate is a "right-now" rulership over the earth's resources. The discovery, reproduction, and manufacturing of the earth's resources for the good of ourselves, our families, and society is a fulfillment of God's will for mankind.

DOMINION CERTIFICATES

In a recent conversation with some businessmen in our church, one of them said to me, "I like to think of money as dominion certificates — nothing more, nothing less." As I leaned forward to hear more, he elaborated on this thought and sent my spirit into orbit. As I heard him talk, I was thinking:

* Money says to land, "You belong to me!"
* Money says to business, " I can own you!"
* Money says to a project, "I will finish you!"
* Money says, "I have the right to rule here and now..."

The more money a person has, the larger his sphere of rulership will be. The less money a person has, the smaller his sphere of rulership will be. Money is the instrument of dominion on the earth. I'll never forget the look on one woman's face as I told her that the Bible says "money answers all things." (Ecclesiastes 10:19) She looked like somebody had

55

slapped her. Although she had been around church for a number of years, she had never heard that scripture before. It was hard for her to imagine that the Bible would credit money with having that much power. It almost seemed blasphemous to her to be saying money answers all things. It seemed to her the Bible would say that prayer or fasting or love answers all things, but surely not money! Most Christians have rightly stated, "The best things in life are free," without stopping to consider that only money can buy everything under the dominion mandate. It's definitely true that money cannot buy love, happiness, peace, or extended life. It's also true, however, that love cannot buy land. Happiness cannot buy a home. Peace won't provide transportation to work, and long life won't pay your living expenses. *So, why do so many people think they have to choose between what money can't buy and what money can buy?* Why not accept the fact that the Bible gives value to both? Let's assume a congregation of believers wants to purchase land and build a building. The fact that they may be a friendly, loving, peaceful, praying congregation doesn't qualify them to take ownership of the land. All their good works are not a dominion certificate that can be exchanged for the land. Money, on the other hand, qualifies them to lay claim to the earth. In our individual lives, our righteousness as Christians places us in right standing with God. However, our righteousness does not give us the right to have ownership of anything in the natural world. Dominion certificates are the recognizable instrument of rulership in the earth.

Whose Earth Is It Anyway?

"The earth is the Lord's and everything in it..."
Psalm 24:1 (NIV)

One of the themes of the great revivals in the early and mid-part of this century was a renouncement of this world. Songs like "I'm a Poor Rich Man," "I'll Fly Away," and "Lately I've Got Leavin' on My Mind," were products of on-fire Christians of that era. Christians were indifferent to the world around them and they saw that as proof of their love for God. Recently, a woman who was watching our TV program wrote me after hearing me reference the "I'll Be Leaving" mentality of Christians. She was so upset! She interpreted what I was saying as a personal attack on the writers and singers of that era. The truth is that I grew up singing some of those songs and hearing those off-the-cuff remarks evangelists would make about this "rotten world" we live in. One of the clichés used most often by preachers in reference to Christians spending time on their home or in their business was "You don't polish brass on a sinking ship" or "No matter how magnificent this world appears, it's just like the Titanic, it's on its way down."

I do realize that these songwriters and preachers meant well and were themselves dedicated and sincere in their faith. But in their zeal to be holy, they promoted "love not the world" (1 John 2:15) without considering "God so loved the world" (John 3:16). In other words, there's a difference in renouncing the evils of the world and renouncing the natural, physical world that God created and Christ died for. It's the same principle of hating sin but loving the sinner. We can hate the sin of the world but love the world for which Christ died. God's word acknowledges our need for houses, food, clothes, and the natural provisions of life. However, God wants us to think beyond that until the whole earth is filled with the knowledge of the glory of the Lord (Habakkuk 2:14) and the kingdoms of the world (corporations, lands, government, buildings, universities) become the kingdoms of our Lord (Revelation 11:15). The presence of evil in the earth is temporary, not eternal. Another reference to this in scripture is the thirty-seventh Psalm.

"Be still before the Lord and wait patiently for him; do not fret when men succeed in their ways, when they carry out their wicked schemes. Refrain from anger and turn from wrath; do not fret – it leads only to evil. For evil men will be cut off, but those who hope in the Lord will inherit the land. A little while, and the wicked will be no more; though you look for them, they will not be

found. But the meek will inherit the land and enjoy great peace." Psalm 37:7-11 (NIV)

So, although the earth has been leased to Satan, the body of Christ has been named the official landlord who will evict him and terminate the lease. The earth is God's; we are His representatives and our assignment is to take back everything Satan has had possession of. Jesus taught his disciples to pray, "Come thy kingdom, be done thy will *ON EARTH* as it is in heaven." This is the goal for which the church was born — to bring the will of God into the earth.

THE TRANSFER OF WEALTH

"The silver is mine and the gold is mine, declares the Lord Almighty." Haggai 2:8 (NIV)

The United States Treasury Department has literally millions of unclaimed dollars that belong to people who are unaware of their fortune. Most of these unclaimed funds are in the form of an inheritance left from a previous generation. The only reason these funds are unclaimed is because people are unaware and have not been notified that the money belongs to them. Just because it's in the possession of the U.S. government, does not mean that it belongs to the U.S. government.

Most Christians assume that the wealth of the world belongs to the "people of the world" since it's in their possession. It's in the bank accounts of Microsoft, IBM, Boeing and other major corporations, so most people assume it's their money. In reality, however, while it's currently in the possession of these companies, it belongs to God and is the inheritance of God's children. *As God's children become aware of their inheritance and make claim on the wealth of the world, it will be surrendered into their hands.*

> *"...to the sinner he gives the task of gathering and storing up wealth to hand it over to the one who pleases God."*
> *Ecclesiastes 2:26 (NIV)*

One couple in our congregation is a tremendous example of our opportunity to lay claim to the wealth of the world. The following is a letter I received from them, sharing their testimony of increase.

> *Shortly after Mom died, my wife and I found ourselves living at poverty level. The Lord led us to begin our own business and we found great help in the positive messages from Pastor Kevin. By applying God's principles to our business, we have prospered beyond our wildest dreams. For example, the income from our business in March, 1997 was over $44,000.00 and in April, 1997 it*

60

was over $56,000.00. Just one month's increase was over $11,000.00 which is more than I was earning per year prior to our present business, which we have been building since March of 1993.

We feel we are just getting started. Our goal is to earn millions so we can give millions to establish God's Kingdom in the Earth. The more we earn the more we give to our church and many other ministries.

We feel very blessed to receive the outstanding teaching of Kevin and Sheila and know that anyone can prosper greatly in every area of their lives by putting these principles into practice. God is no respecter of persons!!

–Anonymous

I get excited when God's people experience increase. In Paul Pilzer's book *God Wants You to Be Rich*, he says:

There are currently over six $100 bills in circulation for every man, woman, and child in the United States — or over twelve $100 bills in circulation for every one of the 128 million people over sixteen years of age in the labor force. The majority of *these 1.57 billion $100 bills are held by drug dealers, vicious criminals, and millions of otherwise ordinary citizens who cheat the rest of us every day by not paying taxes on their incomes.*

In our modern economy, where most law-abiding citizens prefer to use checks and credit cards for most of their financial transactions, the $292 billion of currency in circulation — which includes over $157 billion in $100 bills — represents in large part the savings and the working capital of the underworld and the underground economy.

Confiscating this hoard of savings and working capital would deal a crushing blow to drug dealers from which many would never recover. It would also serve as a powerful deterrent to those non-taxpayers among us who seek to have other citizens pay for the benefits they enjoy in American society. (p.202)

This transfer of wealth is not something that will happen all at once. In fact, it's already started to happen. Everyday, believers are being promoted into better paying jobs, starting and growing successful businesses, and enjoying the prosperity of God in their lives. If you're ready to lay claim to God's gold and silver, there's a book by George S. Clason entitled *The Richest Man in Babylon*. In this book, he reveals five Laws of Gold that I'll list here for your consideration.

THE FIVE LAWS OF GOLD

1. Gold cometh gladly and in increasing quantity to any man who will put not less than one-tenth of his earnings for his future and that of his family.
2. Gold laboreth diligently and contentedly for the wise owner who finds for it profitable employment, multiplying even as the flocks of the field.
3. Gold clingeth to the protection of the cautious owner who invests it under the advice of men wise in its handling.
4. Gold slippeth away from the man who invests it in business or purpose with which he is not familiar or which are not approved by those skilled in its keep.
5. Gold flees the man who would force it to impossible earnings or who followeth the alluring advice of tricksters and schemers or who trusts it to his own inexperience and romantic desires in investment.

These laws are as true today as they were in ancient times.

WHERE I RULE, GOD RULES

Throughout our history we've seen pictures of various

wars where soldiers in U.S. uniforms would occupy territory and post our flag. Famous pictures like Iwo Jima remind us that ordinary soldiers can represent our government and entire nations simply with their presence. These soldiers are commissioned and empowered by our nation to lay claim to the lands and occupy territory on behalf of the United States. When Jesus said, "My kingdom is not of this world," (John 18:36) He was not renouncing His intention to usher God's will into the Earth. He was simply stating that His kingdom did not have *earthly origin*. In fact, He clearly stated He was a king. So, what was the king doing here in the earth and what was He commissioning others to do on His behalf? To occupy territory and extend the kingdom of God into the earth! *The term "Kingdom of God" literally means the "rulership of God." So wherever God rules is God's kingdom.* When some people think of God's kingdom, they limit it to heaven. They think the only place God's kingdom exists is where there are mansions, streets of gold, and eternal life. In reality, wherever God rules is God's kingdom. If God rules in your life, you are kingdom property. If God rules in your house, your house is in the kingdom. If God rules in your business, your business is in the kingdom of God. With that in mind, it's easy to see how the kingdom of God is filling the earth. It's also easy to see our role in taking territory in the form of houses, land, businesses, and stocks to bring them under the rulership of God. We are commissioned and empowered by God to extend His kingdom throughout the earth until all of the earth is under His rulership. The level of "more than enough" prosperity enables us to own businesses, restaurants, newspapers, television programs, radio stations, universities, hospitals, nursing homes — entire communities and cities owned and operated by people who submit to and represent the government of God. Say it with me as you take new territory: "Where I rule, God rules."

"Whoever can be trusted with very little can also be trusted with much..."
Luke 16:10

Chapter 4

THE STEWARDSHIP PRINCIPLE

STEWARDSHIP PRINCIPLE

"Again, it will be like a man going on a journey, who called his servants and entrusted his property to them. To one he gave five talents of money, to another two talents, and to another one talent, each according to his ability. Then he went on his journey. The man who had received the five talents went

at once and put his money to work and gained five more. So also, the one with the two talents gained two more. But the man who had received the one talent went off, dug a hole in the ground and hid his master's money. After a long time the master of those servants returned and settled accounts with them. The man who had received the five talents brought the other five. 'Master,' he said, 'you entrusted me with five talents. See, I have gained five more.' His master replied, 'Well done, good and faithful servant! You have been faithful with a few things; I will put you in charge of many things. Come and share your master's happiness!' The man with the two talents also came. 'Master,' he said, 'you entrusted me with two talents; see, I have gained two more.' His master replied, 'Well done, good and faithful servant! You have been faithful with a few things; I will put you in charge of many things. Come and share your master's happiness!' Then the man who had received the one talent came. 'Master,' he said, 'I knew that you are a hard man, harvesting where you have not sown and gathering where you have not scattered seed. So I was afraid and went out and hid your talent in the ground. See, here is what belongs to you.' His master replied, 'You wicked, lazy servant! So you knew that I harvest where I have not sown and gather where I have not scattered seed? Well then, you should have put my money on deposit with the bankers, so that when I returned I would have received it back with interest. Take the talent from him and give it to the one who has the ten talents. For everyone who has will be given more, and he will have an abundance. Whoever does not have, even what he has will be taken from him. And throw that worthless servant outside, into the darkness, where there will be weeping and gnashing of teeth.' "

Matthew 25:14-27 (NIV)

It's amazing how we can hear something or read something and miss the main point. Many people read, teach, and preach from this parable without really defining the intended message. In fact, my experience has been that more often than not, people misunderstand what biblical stewardship really is. To discover what stewardship is, let's first talk about what stewardship is not.

Stewardship is *not* abstaining from luxuries that provide pleasure. The teaching many Christians have received on stewardship has caused an overemphasis on not "wasting" a dime of your money. Their interpretation, then, is money should not be spent on pleasure items such as taking kids to ball games, fairs, vacations, etc. This guarded approach is sometimes a result of someone's misunderstanding of biblical stewardship, not a result of being unable to afford something.

Stewardship is *not* merely being "frugal." Some people are so focused on clipping out coupons and bargain shopping that they become obsessed with it. Often, they fault others who "pay more" considering themselves to be *wiser* and better stewards. It is interesting to note that, more often than not, those who concentrate heavily on being "thrifty" are also plagued by a poverty mentality. The poverty mentality keeps them from enjoying what they do have because they are so focused on what they *can't afford*.

When it comes to stewardship, the question is not "what do you have?", but rather *"what are you doing with what you have?"* Which leads us to the stewardship principle.

> ### The Stewardship Principle:
> To manage resources in such a way that you increase them.

Looking back at the parable of the talents, the owner gave different amounts of money to each of the three managers. It did not matter that the manager who had received two talents did not bring back as much as the manager who had started with five talents. In fact, the owner commended him with the exact same words as he had the manager who had produced five talents. However, the sharp rebuke (look at it again) to the manager who had not increased his resources went like this. 'Why didn't you at least put the money in the bank so you could earn interest on it?

Every person who reads this book has their own unique circumstances. The one thing we do have in common is God has entrusted all of us with resources. The stewardship principle is to manage resources in such a way that we increase them.

Some people mistakenly think they can do just one thing right and get positive results. For example, when a person wants to lose weight, they can't get results by just *eating* healthy food. They also must *stop* eating *unhealthy* food. Another similar example is that eating healthy doesn't eliminate the risk that comes with smoking. Likewise, *stewardship is the application of multiple principles which together cause increase to happen.* This means we must continually seek strategies of stewardship to add to those we already practice. Below, are three often overlooked strategies of stewardship.

#1 Free Yourself From A "Scarcity" Mentality. The word of God is filled with promises of provision for our lives. However, many of God's people live in constant fear and worry. (This is what caused the manager in Matthew 25 to bury his talent. He was afraid of losing it!) They are afraid of running out of resources. This scarcity mentality is sometimes rooted in the memory of past experiences. Some people who grew up in poverty have a hard time thinking *sufficiency,* much less *abundance.* Even though their financial condition may improve, their minds continue to be stuck in a *mentality of lack.* This scarcity mentality hinders the prosperity of a person's soul as well as their pocket book. It keeps them from giving, sharing, and investing from out of what they do have. *In their mind they have nothing to give, nothing to share, nothing to invest.* The scarcity mentality often goes beyond what we have individually and affects our perception of the world as a whole. The economic doomsayers don't help with their unfounded predictions. They continue to write because there are plenty of people with fear and worry in their hearts who will rush out to buy these kinds of books. Then, when the doomsayer is wrong, nobody holds them accountable for their predictions that didn't come true. Sometimes they simply move forward to write another book based on the same kind of faulty information.

Writers like Ravi Batra, who wrote *The Great Depression of 1990*; (also George Orwell's *1984*; and Paul Erlich's *Population Bomb*) were all best sellers, and they were all *wrong*. Christian doomsayers also exist. Perhaps they are not as well known, but they certainly promote the same kind of false information that reinforces people's fears. In reality, we have every reason to be optimistic about the amount of resources in the world today. Efforts to preserve and multiply our national resources have been successful. Our natural energy reserves such as gold, mercury, tin, zinc, petroleum, copper, lead, and natural gas have actually risen by more than fifty percent from the early 1970s to the early 1990s. God would not create a world with a shortage of resources. It's helpful to look carefully at the terminology of scripture referencing God's provisions for our lives:

"...abundant provision..."
Romans 5:17 (NIV)

"The Lord is my shepherd , I shall not be in want..."
Psalms 23:1 (NIV)

"...a good measure, pressed down,... "
Luke 6:38 (NIV)

"...abounding in every good work."
II Corinthians 9:8 (NIV)

"...sows generously...reaps generously."
II Corinthians 9:6 (NIV)

Yes! God's resources are plentiful and "more than enough."

#2 Set In Motion Your Own Increase By Your Willingness To Decrease. When observing the life-style of a highly paid professional, it is usually not apparent to us that this individual had to *decrease* before they could *increase*. There were college costs that had to be paid *first*. There was time that had to be invested. All this was a "decrease" for them. Some of their friends were not spending the money to go to college, but were getting jobs that didn't require education. Over time, however, the one who decreased for years begins to increase past the level of his peers. This is a spiritual principle that governs life. Decrease is a prerequisite to increase. In Norman Vincent Peale's book *Positive Thinking,* he tells about his own realization of the decrease-to-increase principle.

> *One night I went out alone and walked through Walnut Park near our little apartment, and for the fist time in my life I felt icy terror clutching at my mind and heart. I wasn't just worried; I was terrified. When I finally went home, I could keep it to myself no longer. I said to Ruth, we're in a*

desperate situation, we can't pay the bills. What are we going to do? And her answer really startled me. She said, "We're going to start tithing." "'Tithing?" I echoed. "Tithing with what? We can't do it. It's impossible!" "No," Ruth said. "Not impossible. Essential. You know what the Bible promises to those who give ten percent of everything to the Lord." I can see her yet, standing right there in the kitchen and quoting Malachi 3:10 to me: 'Bring ye all the tithes into the storehouse... and prove me now herewith, said the Lord of hosts, if I will not open you the windows of heaven, and pour you out a blessing, that there shall not be room enough to receive it. We're going to do that, she said stoutly, and we're not going to starve, either. We're not going to be evicted. We are going to get by on ninety percent of your twice cut salary because tithing is an act of faith, and the Bible says that 'if we have faith even as small as a grain of mustard seed, nothing will be impossible for us. We have to start imagining God's prosperity. So we did it and Ruth was right, we did get by. Money certainly didn't pour in but there always was just enough. Furthermore; the act of tithing seemed to calm my fears and stimulate my mind so that I began thinking. I started imagining. I knew I had one small talent: public speaking. And so I decided to try to capitalize on that. I offered myself as a public speaker whenever one was *needed. I spoke at civic clubs and garden clubs and graduations and community gatherings. Sometimes I was paid five or ten dollars, sometimes nothing at all, but it helped. What a thrill I felt when I received the first twenty-five dollar fee. Then someone who heard me speak offered me a chance to go on radio. Again there was no money for this, but the number of speaking invitations increased. So one thing led to another; and gradually we began to get our heads above water. I am convinced that tithing did it. Anyway, Ruth and I have been tithers ever since, and there is something about this practice of giving that can't be explained in purely rational terms.*

Not only does this principle of decreasing to increase apply when tithing, but it should also be observed in giving and investing. Many people fail to set any increase in motion because they are unwilling to *let go* of what is in their hand. I'm not advocating throwing your money at anyone and anything that comes along, but I am encouraging you to take calculated risks by seeking investment opportunities that will put your money to work for you. An unknown millionaire tells how he made his fortune.

It was really quite simple. I bought an apple for five cents, spent the whole evening polishing it, and sold it the next day for ten cents. With this I bought two apples, spent the evening polishing them and sold them for twenty cents. And so it went until I had amassed a few thousand dollars. It was then that I bought shares in Apple Computer Corporation and made ten million dollars.

Notice how the journey of financial growth required periodic seasons of decrease. The first apple, the reinvestment in apples, and then the reinvestment of the thousands that represented hours of work. Jesus says it like this:

"Give, and it will be given to you. A good measure, pressed down, shaken together and running over, will be poured into your lap. For with the measure you use, it will be measured to you."
Luke 6:38 (NIV)

This strategy of stewardship governs all of life, not just finances. If you are in a season of decrease, don't allow yourself to be discouraged. *If you are giving, saving, and investing according to the word of God, increase is on its way.* As the apostle Paul says:

"Let us not become weary in doing good, for at the proper time we will reap a harvest if we do not give up." Galatians 6:9 (NIV)

 # 3 Focus On Your Personal Potential For Increase. Your resources are much more than the amount of dollars you have to your name. Biblical success begins on the inside of us. Because our culture is so *exterior* oriented, we often have to have a paradigm shift before we can discover our personal potential for increase. Let's look at four potentials within all of us.

Earning Potential. One misconception about millionaires is that they are all like Mr. Howell on Gilligan's Island — a person with a stuffy personality who never worked a day in his life. This misconception is that everyone who is wealthy inherits their wealth and doesn't know anything about "real life." The truth, however, is that many of today's millionaires are ordinary individuals. Research shows that they are usually self-made, live a normal life-style, own their own business, and stay involved in it daily. They have been married a long time to the same person and attend church regularly. There are over a million of these kinds of millionaires living in America today. What this tells us is that there are unlimited opportunities to earn.

Another misconception is that wealthy people are solely interested in making money, and will do whatever necessary to make a buck. My experience has been that most successful earners are passionate about their life's work. They are genuinely inspired to not only do their work, but to do it with excellence. These people literally enjoy what they do and view it as their contribution to the world. They have tapped into and developed their earning potential. Failure to use your earning potential results in a life-style of lack.

"For you yourselves know how you ought to follow our example. We were not idle when we were with you, nor did we eat anyone's food without paying for it. On the contrary, we worked night and day, laboring and toiling so that we would not be a burden to any of you. We did this, not because we do not have the right to such help, but in order to make ourselves a model for you to follow. For even when we were with you, we gave you this rule: "If a man will not work, he shall not eat."
II Thessalonians 3:7-10

Sometimes, people are in jobs that offer little hope for increase. In some situations it's wise to consider second business opportunities. There are many legitimate businesses that don't require a lot of extra time and energy. I've seen this work well for people who wanted to increase their income to pay for their children's college tuition, a down payment on homes, and retirement funds.

Management Potential. Too often, people manage on a crisis basis. In other words, they only manage life as a reaction to circumstances. The result is that the most important goals of their life are always delayed by the urgent, less important demands placed on them. Learn to allocate time, energy, attention, and finances to the things you care most about. *The ability to choose what matters most and put our resources into it is a management potential we all possess.* People who deny their management potential may make a lot of money and then lose their family. What good is the money if the people you love most aren't in your life? I now put my family time, prayer time, study time, play time, and exercise time on my calendar. I used to only put meetings on my schedule. Then I realized I wasn't setting aside time for things that mattered most. Now my most important events go on *first*. This willingness to manage by priority will put your resources in alignment with what matters most. Everyone has management potential in their life. Put it to work for you today.

Planning Potential Different people want different things. What do you and your spouse want most? Notice I included your spouse in this. The reason is often what is most important to us, may not be most important to them. It only takes a short list to begin to see where we may differ on what we want most.

- Cash reserves
- Insurance
- College for children
- Retirement
- Vacations/travel
- Percentage of giving
- Automobiles
- House

Remember, this *want* list assumes we first want God's presence in our lives and happiness in our home. Having that, what do we want to do most with the money we will earn now and in the future? Often, financial planners, relatives, and other people tell us what we should prioritize. I've even had members of our church tell me that their banker or CPA was telling them they shouldn't tithe or give like they do. When it's time to plan for your future, let God's word dictate what you want most. Some people may criticize you for going on vacation and see it as a waste of money. Other people won't share your value of owning your own home. What is wasteful to some is valuable to others. We should always keep our minds receptive to wisdom regarding our finances. However, within the realm of wisdom, planning is a matter of personal preference.

Investment Potential Investment strategies change with circumstances, but everyone has investment potential. My observation is that our investment potential begins in something other than stocks, IRA's and mutual funds. Our investment potential begins with our investment in ourselves. Decisions to increase education, improve skills, enlarge vocabulary, enhance personal appearance, learn a trade, be physically fit, eat sensibly, pray daily, and read regularly are foundational investment choices. The self investments are important because you are the "earner." Some people are like the farmer grabbing for the golden egg while neglecting to feed the goose who laid it. I'm a strong believer in guarding against personal burnout, spiritual starvation or mental fatigue. The way to prevent this is to invest continually in yourself. If you owned a valuable automobile you wouldn't put ketchup in the oil tank. You wouldn't leave it out in the weather — not if you wanted maximum potential and value. Why is it that so many people treat their automobiles or pets better than themselves?

Another observation of investment is that my best choices for investment may not be the best choices for someone else. For example, I don't invest much in tools. I'm not a handyman. I mess things up when I try to fix them, so tools are not a good investment for me. For some men, however, it is a wise investment for them to put thousands of dollars into tools. As a minister, I'm on a different set of tax rules than most people. One of my best investments is in my home. Everyone's investment scenarios may vary, but everyone has investment potential. Since I'm a novice myself, I don't want to go deeply into financial investment strategies. However, I would like to encourage you to consider the importance of investing. A friend of mine told me recently that an investment of $25,000 has become almost $500,000 in just twelve years. This investment required no energy from him to make it multiply. This is the beauty of the many investment opportunities available to us. It's called "passive productivity." You do nothing except invest in a successful, growing enterprise, and your money works for you multiplying over and over again.

When some people think of investing their money, they only think of stocks, bonds, and mutual funds. I like to think of buying gifts for my wife as an important investment in my marriage. When we plan our vacation, we think of it as making memories that are well worth a financial investment. Recently, a member of our staff told me about a financial decision he and his wife had made. For some time, they had planned to build a nice garage on their property. They saw it as a functional need for automobiles, lawn mowers and other assets they owned. At the same time, they had entertained the thought of buying a boat that they could have fun in as a family. Since they didn't feel like they could afford both at the same time, they were forced to decide between the two. Their decision to buy the boat would be considered by some people as a less important investment. After all, the boat would depreciate in value and the garage would enhance their property value. Their reasoning, however, was that their sons (ages thirteen and fifteen) would enjoy the boat a lot more, and it would facilitate some great family time. I applauded them for this decision to invest in their family relationships. It was exciting to hear them talk about how much fun they were all having together on their boat. The comment this staff member made that sticks out in my mind was, "My garage can wait, but my boys will never be thirteen and fifteen again." Remember it's not foolish to invest in your self, your marriage, or your children. Give yourself permission to put money into things and events that improve yourself and enhance relationships with those you love.

"THE GREATEST OF EVILS AND THE WORST OF CRIMES IS POVERTY...OUR FIRST DUTY, A DUTY TO WHICH EVERY OTHER CONSIDERATION SHOULD BE SACRIFICED, IS NOT TO BE POOR."

—GEORGE BERNARD SHAW

Chapter 5

THE WEALTH OF WISDOM

OPPOSING POVERTY

As you read this book, perhaps you or someone you know is under extreme financial pressure. Monetary insufficiency and lack create tremendous stress. People do irrational things when the dictating power of poverty imposes its will upon its victims. The number one reason given for divorce is financial problems. The need for money is the motivation for most crimes. From embezzlement to prostitution, poverty is the common thread of evil. So why are so many people passive about poverty? Why are so many Christians comfortable in the presence of this enemy? Some people who are quick to stand up against other forms of evil are extremely tolerant of the ongoing, never-ending presence of poverty in their life. It's important to pull the mask off of this degrading, threatening, enslaving power called poverty and regard it as an enemy.

Webster's dictionary defines poverty as "the condition of being poor or needy"; A deficiency in necessary properties; inadequacy; scarcity." It is obvious when reading scripture that God's *promises* and *plans* for our lives are in direct conflict with the condition of poverty.

THE WEALTH OF WISDOM

So many times people want to change their financial status without changing their thoughts or actions. These people fail to realize that thinking the same way and doing the same thing is going to give them the same results. *The foundational attitude for opposing poverty is the ongoing pursuit of wisdom.* An open mind that is hungry for new thoughts and willing to change is the foundation for never-ending prosperity.

"With me (wisdom) are riches and honor,
enduring wealth and prosperity."
Proverbs 8:18 (NIV)

Lack and insufficiency are signs that something needs to change. It is amazing how many people resist the very change that is a key to their breakthrough. They turn away from wisdom's voice and continue to struggle. Until you genuinely believe in your heart that the challenge of the change is less painful than the continuation of your struggle, you won't change your financial status. Let me say it this way: the premise for change is to enlarge our capacity for increase. Resistance to that change keeps our capacity where it is. We see it in corporate America continually. Secretaries who resist learning to operate computers are finding themselves unable to increase their salaries. So it is with any employee who resists change and adjustment in our ever-changing world. They will always find themselves decreasing in value to their employer. In Genesis 13, Abraham released his potential for increase after he and his nephew Lot had hit a ceiling. Unless they made a change, they would not see increase. In fact, they were already experiencing what could lead to a decline because of strife among their servants. It was time to hear the voice of wisdom. The change would not be easy, but it was necessary for prosperity to continue.

"But the land could not support them while they stayed together, for their possessions were so great that they were not able to stay together. And quarreling arose between Abram's herdsmen and the herdsmen of Lot. So Abram said to Lot, 'Let's not have any quarreling between you and me, or between your herdsmen and mine, for we are brothers. Is not the whole land before you? Let's part company. If you go to the left, I'll go to the right; if you go to the right, I'll go to the left.' "
Genesis 13:6-9 (NIV)

When it comes to financial increase, remember that the same level of thinking that got you where you are won't take you where you want to go. Wisdom's voice may recommend difficult changes. Wisdom's voice may insist that you further your education. Wisdom's voice may say to invest in your personal appearance when you don't really want to buy clothes. Wisdom's voice may tell you to begin saving so you can start a business. Wisdom will not always say what we want to hear, but with wisdom is lasting wealth and prosperity. The willingness to welcome wisdom is the first step to changing our financial status.

The book of Proverbs was written by the wisest man that ever lived and his staff of insightful writers. The following chapters of "proverbs that oppose poverty" will serve to help set our course in the direction of prosperity.

"BUT SEEK FIRST HIS KINGDOM AND HIS RIGHTEOUSNESS, AND ALL THESE THINGS WILL BE GIVEN TO YOU AS WELL."
MATTHEW 6:33

Chapter 6

OPPOSING POVERTY PROVERB #1

Opposing Poverty Proverb #1
Prioritize God's Kingdom.

"Honor the Lord with your wealth, with the first fruits of all your crops; then your barns will be filled to overflowing, and your vats will brim over with new wine." Proverbs 3:9-10 (NIV)

The practice of giving the first ten percent of all increase began in Hebrew history before the time of the Mosaic law. The first recorded instances of tithing in the Bible occur in the book of Genesis. In the first setting, Abraham brought his tithe to Melchizedek, the priest of God. In the second recorded instance, Jacob made a lifelong tithing commitment.

"After Abram returned from defeating Kedorlaomer and the kings allied with him, the king of Sodom came out to meet him in the Valley of Shaveh (that is, the King's Valley). Then Melchizedek king of Salem brought out bread and wine. He was priest of God Most High, and he blessed Abram, saying, 'Blessed be Abram by God Most High, Creator of heaven and earth. And blessed be God Most High, who delivered your enemies into your hand.' Then Abram gave him a tenth of everything." Genesis 14:17-20 (NIV)

"Then Jacob made a vow, saying, 'If God will be with me and will watch over me on this journey I am taking and will give me food to eat and clothes to wear so that I return safely to my father's house, then the Lord will be my God and this stone that I have set up as a pillar will be God's house, and of all that you give me I will give you a tenth.' " Genesis 28:20-22 (NIV)

It's important to not confuse the act of tithing with other Old Testament rituals originating under the law. Tithing was introduced long before the law and is an affirmation of faith in God. The covenant of tithing is one of the keys to opposing poverty because it redeems and protects our property from the curse of poverty. The biblical principle of redeeming our goods from the curse of poverty occurs when we tithe. In other words, the ten percent redeems the ninety percent. When we bring our tithe, we are protecting the rest of our possessions. Remember the Allstate commercial "You're in good hands with Allstate"? The same is true for us when we tithe. We literally put our possessions in God's hands when we tithe. This method of redeeming is something God has done throughout history. This is what prompted the bringing of lambs, turtledoves and other animals for sacrifice. By bringing the *first* of the herd, flock or crop, God's people would invoke God's covering over their remaining possessions. Anything not redeemed was considered to be under the Genesis curse. In Leviticus, God even told them that if they were not going to redeem a donkey; they should break its neck. The act of redeeming is what our salvation rests upon. Faith for the redeeming of our possessions from the curse is exactly the same method as faith for the redeeming of our lives by Christ's death. He was the first who redeems the rest! I not only pray God's covering over my possessions; I activate God's covering through tithing.

"And I will rebuke the devourer for your sakes, and he shall not destroy the fruits of your ground; neither

shall your vine cast her fruit before the time in the field,
saith the Lord of hosts?" Malachi 3:11 (KJV)

Notice the promise of God is that he will "rebuke" the devourer. What a word picture! Imagine God's host standing *guard* over your possessions. Can you see God's hedge of protection? God's umbrella covering your house, land and finances? If you are a tither, that's exactly what you have. Your goods are in God's hands.

Do I Tithe On Net Or Gross?

Business owners often wonder what God expects them to tithe on. After all, they have the cost of doing business. There are initial investments and sometimes the business has more expenses than income. No one scripture addresses this better than this one in the Amplified Version:

"Honor the Lord with your capital and
sufficiency from righteous labors and with
the firstfruits of all your income."
Proverbs 3:9 (AMP)

The first thing this scripture references is our *capital.* Capital is the total increase minus total expenses. If you buy a house for $80,000 invest $20,000 and then sell it for $130,000, the capital increase is $30,000. If you invest $5,000 in stock and later sell it for $12,000 the capital increase is $7,000. I tithe on capital increase in addition to tithing on income. The reason this is so important to note is because good money managers will often find creative ways to bring home less money than they are actually making. There are legal ways to structure income so that business owners shelter themselves from heavy taxation. There is nothing wrong with this if it is legal and moral. It does, however, cause some people to deny God the full tithe. The intention may not be to rob God, but that is the result. Tithing is only tithing if it is a full ten percent of all increase. God is not the IRS. He is your provider. He does not want you to play cat-and-mouse games. He wants us to acknowledge all (the full amount) of our increase by tithing on it. As for our personal income, it's all an increase to us and should be tithed on. The second part of the above verse says "...and the first fruit of all your income." **The reason I tithe on my gross income is because the taxes I pay benefit me. In an indirect way, it's an increase to me.**

Tithing Is A New Testament Principle

Hebrews 7 gives great insight into the tithing principle. Some people get confused because of the wording in Hebrews 7, as it relates to tithing. To help make it clear, first read verses one through eleven, then I'll give you information that should bring clarity to this scripture and its teaching. At the very least, tithing is assumed in the New Testament. The words tithe and tithing appear eight times between Matthew and Hebrews. (Matthew 23:23, Luke 11:42, 18:12, Hebrews 7:5-6, 8-9) All of these passages confirm and endorse the practice of tithing. If anything, the New Testament encourages giving to go beyond the tithe as a way to receive a harvest of blessing and prosperity.

1. Melchizedek was both a king and a priest in the days of Abraham before the giving of the law. (Hebrews 7:1)
2. Melchizedek blessed Abraham and Abraham gave his tithe to him. (Hebrews 7:1- 2)
3. The priests, who were sons of Levi, were under commandment to take tithes of the people who descended from Abraham (Hebrews 7:5)
4. There is a likeness in the Melchizedek order and the Christ order of priesthood. (Hebrews 7:6-10)

   ◆ Melchizedek was "outside" the law, as is Christ's priesthood.
   ◆ Melchizedek was both king and priest, so is Christ.
   ◆ Neither were of Aaron's priesthood nor lineage.
   ◆ Tithing is an obligation in both priesthoods. (Matthew 23:23)

5. A greater priesthood exists after the order of the new covenant than was under the law (Hebrews 7: 11).

- ◆ Should an earthly priesthood receive tithe and not the eternal/greater priesthood?
- ◆ The need for which tithing was implemented has not ceased.

When we practice the principle of tithing, we acknowledge God as our source, and we make a statement against poverty. The fact that we give the tithe confirms our expectation of God's provision in our lives. It's acting on our belief of abundance.

I consistently receive letters of testimony thanking me for teaching the financial principles of the Bible. Recently in one letter, a couple in our church shared with me how God had provided dramatically for them and answered their prayers. As I read the letter, I was reminded of the day they came to me several years ago and were making a career transition. I encouraged them to be committed to the tithe principle although they were about to lose their home and everything they had. It was not an easy road, but the last paragraph of their letter tells it all.

From the day you counseled us when we left our former career to begin all over at our age, almost losing our home and wondering where and what we should do, we have come to a time of blessing. Kevin, never stop telling our church family to bring the full tithe into the storehouse. We can never out-give God. He is a God we can trust.

It is in situations like these where a couple has remained faithful in difficult times that "proves God". (Malachi 3:10) Now they are both enjoying new and prosperous careers. The tithe is the instrument of covenant with God that acknowledges Him as our constant, never failing source of provision. As we stay faithful to the covenant, He is committed to our success. He will take us down a path that will ultimately lead us to places of abundant provision. On our journey, He will sustain us and always supply our need, but ultimately He is looking to put every tither under the "open windows" of promise. It's under the open windows and floodgates of heaven where He pours out so much blessing that we don't have enough room to receive it. (Malachi 3:10)

GIVING GOD YOUR BEST BY PUTTING FIRST THINGS FIRST How does God intend to make sure we continually prioritize the expansion of His kingdom? What does He expect from us when our lives begin to prosper? This is not only a legitimate concern for us in our generation, but has been a factor in the prosperity of God's people throughout time. Read carefully the instruction given to the people of Israel when God was leading them into greater prosperity.

"When you have eaten and are satisfied, praise the Lord your God for the good land He has given you. Be careful that you do not forget the Lord your God, failing to observe his commands, his laws and his decrees that I am giving you this day. Otherwise, when you eat and are satisfied, when you build fine houses and settle down, and when your herds and flocks grow large and your silver and gold increase and all you have is multiplied, then your heart will become proud and you will forget the Lord your God, who brought you out of Egypt . You will become proud and you will forget the Lord your God, who brought you out of Egypt you will become proud and will forget the land of slavery."
Deuteronomy 8:10-14 (NIV)

Notice the instruction carefully. *There is no insinuation that God is displeased with their having good land, fine houses, large herds, increased silver, and multiplied gold.* In fact, God gave it to them! The warning, however, is that when you have these things, be sure you don't forget the Lord your God, or fail to observe His commands, laws, and decrees. This concern continues to be expressed a few verses later.

"You may say to yourself 'My power and the strength of my hands have produced this wealth for me.' But remember the Lord your God, for it is he who gives you the ability to produce wealth, and so confirms his covenant, which he swore to your forefathers, as it is today."
Deuteronomy 8:17-18 (NIV)

Again, notice carefully God is not opposed to them having wealth. In fact, He wants them to know that whatever they accumulate when they prosper is because He empowered them with the ability to produce wealth. It's obvious, however, that God wants them to remember Him as their source.

God sees that what we do first with our money is an indication of what is first in our lives. Although some people know that Malachi 3 commands us to "bring all the tithe into the storehouse" (v.10), what they fail to realize is that this command comes on the heels of a heated rebuke in Malachi 1. In fact, it's fair to say God was "ticked" at His people because they failed to give Him proper respect in their giving habits. This setting gives insight into God's association of giving habits and honoring Him. He's seeing their careless giving as an indication that they are not putting Him first in their lives.

"A son honors his father, a servant his master...where's their respect due me, says the Lord?"
Malachi 1:6

"When you bring blind animals for sacrifice, is that not wrong? When you sacrifice crippled or diseased animals is that not wrong? Try offering them to the governor! Would he be pleased with you? Would he accept you? says the Lord?"
Malachi 1:8

(Verse 14) "Cursed is the cheat who has an acceptable male in his flock and vows to give it, but then sacrifices a blemished animal...For I am a great king," says the Lord Almighty...
Malachi 1:14

Is He upset or what? He's totally insulted by the fact that people who claim to be His people are bringing Him less than their best. Like an attorney hammering his point in a courtroom, God says "you wouldn't treat your dinner guest like you're treating me...stop bringing me the crippled, blind, imperfect sacrifices that are not worth much to you... Don't bring me your *leftovers*. I deserve your best and nothing less!" Go God!

This is the heart and soul of tithing. The *first fruit* is a reference to prioritizing and putting God first.

In this setting of Malachi, God also charges them with *contempt.* We are most familiar with this word in association with our judicial system. To be in "contempt of court" is to have an attitude of resistance to the court. In other words, God was pointing out a resistance in the people when it came to giving Him their best. The indication was that they wanted to appease Him to His face, but slyly resisted giving Him what they wanted to keep for themselves.

TITHING IS DESIGNATED FOR THE CHURCH WHERE YOU WORSHIP The tithe is a first fruit. This *designated* portion is considered a tithe only when it arrives in the treasury of the "storehouse" (church) where we receive our spiritual nourishment.

"Bring the whole tithe into the storehouse,
that there may be food in my house."
Malachi 3:10 (NIV)

The specific recipient of the tithe is the office of the priesthood. It's a practical and reasonable obligation to those who do the work of ministry. The tithe enables the ministry to prepare and provide what men, women, children, and youth need to learn and grow in their relationship with God. A person who receives their groceries at one store would not consider going to another store to pay for them. Just because they sent a payment to one department store chain, they would not assume they could go to another chain and leave without paying. That's exactly what believers do when they send money to charities and count it as a tithe. They go to their church on Sunday morning, receive the ministry provided by the pastor and staff and want to count what they sent to the "March of Dimes" as tithe.

There are many worthwhile charities to give to, but the tithe is not *credited* as being received until it arrives in the church treasury. The church is the only designated recipient of the tithe, and the priesthood is the only group of individuals authorized by God to receive the tithe from men.

"ALL LABOR THAT UPLIFTS HUMANITY HAS DIGNITY AND IMPORTANCE AND SHOULD BE UNDERTAKEN WITH PAINSTAKING EXCELLENCE."
—MARTIN LUTHER KING JR.

Chapter 7

Opposing Poverty Proverb #2

> **Opposing poverty proverb #2**
> **Be committed to your life work.**

In 1964, President Johnson declared war on poverty. Unfortunately, instead of leading America into productivity and a stronger work ethic he did the exact opposite. He started welfare programs. In the next fifteen years:

- The welfare budget increased from 2 billion to 185 billion dollars.

- Welfare recipients went from 500,000 to 22 million.

When people lose their commitment to work, poverty increases.

"Go to the ant, you sluggard; consider its ways and be wise! It has no commander, no overseer or ruler, yet it stores its provisions in the summer and gathers its food at harvest. How long will you lie there, you sluggard? When will you get up from your sleep? A little sleep, a little slumber, a little folding of the hands to rest and poverty will come on you like a bandit and scarcity like an armed man." Proverbs 6:6-11 (NIV)

For the Christian, the marketplace is more than a job — it's a place to serve and glorify God. The Bible refers to the occupations of people as an important part of their life. Throughout scripture God's people were people of worthwhile occupations:

- blacksmiths
- farmers
- soldiers
- fishermen
- homemakers
- doctors
- sales people
- business owners
- tax collectors

Employment is the marketplace of today's society. It's the center of activity, trade, and interaction. The assumption of some Christians is that their life work has no spiritual significance. They have a concept that only people in full-time ministry are working for the Lord. The Bible teaches otherwise.

"Whatever you do, work at it with all of your heart, as working for the Lord, not for men,..."
Colossians 3:23 (NIV)

Whatever you do. If you're an accountant, work those numbers and those budgets as a work of great value unto God. If you're a plumber, repair those pipes with great enthusiasm as a work unto the Lord.

Work at it with all your heart. Put your heart into it! If you're a school teacher, see the incredible opportunity you have as a work with Godly purpose. If you're building houses, don't compromise quality, thinking it's not important. Put your heart into it as the work God has given you to do.

People who see themselves as merely working to "get by" seem to always produce mediocre results. On the other hand, people who approach work as their own valuable contribution to society experience greater success. The ambition to provide a service to society that is meaningful enough to get you up in the morning and keep you moving all day, is the highest and best purpose for work. When your life's work is reduced to "making a living", all you will get is a living and not much else. There will be little fulfillment and joy in your days and eventually the quality of life and work will decline.

In a recent survey, managers were asked what they dislike most in the people they supervise. Here are the top nine frustrations listed in *Success Secrets* by Merrill Douglas:

1. **Procrastinating instead of acting on things.** When a manager or supervisor asks you to do something, ask for the time frame and deliver. Time loss means financial loss to a company. That's why it's important to be prompt and quick to respond to given tasks and responsibilities.
2. **Passing the buck.** As seen by a supervisor, an employee's willingness to assume responsibility is a positive attribute to a supervisor. People who assume responsibility for getting a job done, always increase their value to an organization.
3. **Claiming to know how to do something and then messing it up.** If you don't know how, admit it and ask to be shown. It doesn't make you look incapable unless you pretend to know how to do something, and then don't perform it, or perform it poorly.
4. **Doing the absolute minimum expected instead of doing the extra to excel.** Phrases like "that's not my job" should be eliminated from your

thoughts if it's a job you can do that will benefit your employer. Nike's phrase "Just do it" is a slogan of all champions, even those in the marketplace.

5. **Delivering sloppy or unfinished work.** It costs an employer time and money to correct mistakes and errors in judgment. Most supervisors know you're human, but must guard against having to do the same job more than once because it is unacceptable or incomplete.

6. **Trying to work beyond their abilities.** This frustration is usually a result of a person wanting to "do it all," for fear of being outshined by someone else who can do something better than they can.

7. **Regularly going over the boss's head.** When an employee does this, they may win an occasional battle, but they will eventually lose the war. Learn to work directly with supervisors.

8. **Constantly engaging in personal conversation, gossiping, and idle socializing.** Don't bring personal problems, personal information, or negative talk into the workplace.

9. **Laziness.** The ability to see what needs to be done without being told, is a key ingredient to gaining the favor of a supervisor. Lazy people don't consider themselves unwilling to work, they just don't have a mind focused on getting things done.

Never doubt that God promotes people when their attitudes and actions in the marketplace are pleasing to Him. In Genesis 31:6-9; Jacob was repeatedly mistreated by the man he worked for, but God saw Jacob's ethics in business matters and continued to promote him until Jacob became independently wealthy.

The world's approach to getting ahead is usually inconsiderate and unethical. Christians who want to succeed in the marketplace should approach their careers with a commitment to excellence. A commitment to excellence does not change because other people compromise ethics and integrity in the workplace. Some Christians mistakenly assume that to do business in the *real world*, a person has to use the questionable tricks-of-the-trade. Unless a person resolves within themselves to embrace ethical excellence, compromise is inevitable. The reason is that unless you're motivated to be true to yourself, you will lack the determination to be true to others. Most people know the obvious ethical violations that occur in the manners of today's marketplace. Part of personal excellence is to hold yourself to a standard that insists on excellent marketplace manners.

BAD MARKETPLACE MANNERS

To be unpredictable in your mood. It's impossible to enjoy working with moody people. Moody people are miserable, and want everyone else to be miserable with them. Misery loves company.

To be self-righteous. Because a person is a Christian doesn't automatically make them superior in the marketplace. Christians sometimes get it in their heads that they don't want to work around "swearing, smoking, fornicating sinners." This self-righteous attitude creates tension and is a bad marketplace mannerism.

To create win-lose situations. It's unfortunate when people on the same team become adversarial. People with high standards of excellence are dissatisfied with anything less than win-win.

To delegate upward. Some people are especially good at taking problems on a specific assignment to their boss to solve for them. The boss, who may be too busy to think it through, will take responsibility for solving a problem that should have never come to him.

To not show appreciation. It's easy to take our jobs for granted, and focus attention on what we dislike. The drive, the hours, the atmosphere, rather than what is good about our jobs.

To be unteachable. This bad manner is usually rooted in a resistance to authority. Sometimes it began in childhood, when an overbearing parent caused a child to promise themselves "someday, nobody will tell me what to do." Now, as an adult, that person is difficult to teach.

Og Mandino said, "The only certain measure of success is to render more and better service than expected. If you want job security, make it your goal to be worth more than your salary. People who only do what they are paid to do are not earning an increase."

"...It is more blessed to give than to receive."
Acts 20:35

Chapter 8

OPPOSING POVERTY PROVERB #3

> Opposing Poverty Proverb #3
> **Be generous and liberal in your giving.**

"One man gives freely, yet gains even more; another
withholds unduly, but comes to poverty.
A generous man will prosper;
he who refreshes others will himself be refreshed."
Proverbs 11:24-25 (NIV)

Billy Graham says, "God has given us two hands, one
with which to give and the other with which to receive."
This is a true statement. Unless you give, you will

not receive. In the same way, if your hand is not open, God will not fill it. It is those people who are constantly sowing seeds that are given more seeds to sow. The answer to lack is not holding back. We need to set the church free from the spirit of *holding back*. In our church we have an annual offering that we call "Liberty Offering." Although we use the offering proceeds for maintaining and upgrading our facilities, the main emphasis of the offering is on *sacrificial giving*. It is an opportunity for us to involve entire families, adults, children, and youth in a concentrated, unified effort of giving. What our church has discovered is that there is a tremendous *high* in doing what it takes to reach the level of sacrificial giving. People work overtime to participate. Young people do odd jobs, baby-sitting, etc. to participate. Families have garage sales, sometimes selling items of value to give in the "Liberty offering." It's our way of standing up against the feeling of "I can't afford to give." We have seen time and again so many breakthroughs in people's individual lives when they gave in this manner. Here is one of my favorite testimonies of blessing in a time of potential disaster.

Dear Kevin,

The day before our Liberty offering my husband got a call from the president of his company telling

118

him that five of the sales representatives in the company had resigned and started their own company. Because they took vendors with them, this translated into a potential loss of major income for us. During the Sunday service my husband and I both felt impressed to give more than we had originally planned. We wanted our offering to be sacrificial so we gave 50% more. On Monday morning, the president called my husband and thanked him for his attitude and loyalty. On Friday a letter came and my husband received a promotion and a $9,000.00 a year raise. We were really blown away!

Sincerely Blessed!

What Happens When We Give?

Most people realize that it is good to give, but don't really know what happens when we give. Below are six things that happen when we give.

1. We prove our priorities through our giving habits. It's one thing to say "God is first." It is another thing to prioritize where we give our money as a confirmation that God is first in our life. When we step up from token giving to liberal giving we prove our priorities. In Haggai 1, the preacher challenged the people to prioritize God's house. He called on them to discontinue investing in their own homes and letting the temple remain in ruins. They responded to his teaching and gave liberally to the needs of the house of God. The message is clear, "take care of God's house and he will take care of yours."

2. We free ourselves from the love of money. Good giving habits keep us "loose" from money's grip. The love of money has little to do with how much you have. Oftentimes, people with little have a hard time giving because they don't have more. People with lots, sometimes have trouble giving because they have trained themselves to save. Keeping your hand open in a consistent pattern of giving will keep money from having a hold on you.

3. We communicate our trust in God. Giving says "God is my provider." Giving proclaims "my God shall supply all my need." When people are insecure and not fully persuaded that God will provide they are reluctant to give.

4. We conquer containment by sowing seeds that will cause a harvest. This is especially true in giving offerings. Remember "tithe for protection, offerings for progression." When we give offerings, we sow seeds to move us beyond the place where we presently are. It's not uncommon to have a "*lid*" on your life. When a lid is there, it's telling you that you can't go any higher. Often, people express a feeling of containment, as if progress is impossible. Giving is a tool that conquers containment.

5. We facilitate the growth of God's kingdom. When we give we are contributing to the expansion of God's kingdom in the Earth. If you are not giving, you are not contributing to growth. In fact, others are paying your way! Liberal givers "pay their way" and give enough to finance TV programs, signs, buildings, and staff so that others can be reached and taught. Liberal givers understand that a church's progress is directly related to the giving of the people.

6. We obey God's instruction for our lives. Perhaps this is the most important thing that happens when we give. God loves cheerful givers (2 Corinthians 9:7). Nothing demonstrates *ongoing obedience* any better than consistent giving. As a pastor, I have seen tremendous blessing come to our church financially. We once received a $250,000 write-off from a lender who created an incentive for us to pay off one loan early. We have overcome tremendous adversity. It is no doubt that the obedience of our congregation has been a key to God's favor on us.

WHAT IS AN OFFERING?

Offerings are not tithes, and tithes are not offerings. Some people assume that their tithe is the sum total of all their charitable giving. These people add the

2% they gave to the children's hospital to the 4% they gave to the needy family members to the 2% they gave to a youth missions trip to the 2% they put in the offering at church and call this their tithe. The fact is, however, that the only part of their giving that could possibly qualify as the tithe is the 2% they gave to their church. The tithe is designated for the specific purpose of establishing and growing the church (Malachi 3:10). Offerings, on the other hand, are discretionary funds given in any amount to the church and other worthwhile causes. If tithing was the sum total of all charitable giving, the word *offering* would never need to appear in the Bible. It would be considered the "tithe." Offering does appear, however, repeatedly in scripture. Offerings are properly defined as the willful, voluntary giving that we do above and beyond our tithe.

Giving Is An Attitude
The goal in giving is to give liberally (Proverbs 11:24, 25) and cheerfully (II Corinthians 9:7). Giving has as much to do with "how" we give as it does with "what" we give. When Jesus said "give and it will be given unto you," (Luke 6:38) He was providing us with a visual concept of how giving initiates an eventual, undeniable return back into our lives. I have found it helpful to allow these words to break down selfish tendencies. I do this by continually positioning myself as a cheerful, zealous giver in my attitude. I remind

myself when I sense reluctance towards giving that *I'm a big giver, and big givers are big receivers.*

"Remember this: Whoever sows sparingly will also reap sparingly, and whoever sows generously will also reap generously."
II Corinthians 9:6 (NIV)

In Genesis 17, God introduced himself to Abram as "El-shaddai" which means "the God of more than enough." He was saying to Abram, this is how I want you to know Me — as the God of more than enough. He did not say to Abram "I'm El-stingi". He said I'm El-shaddai — a giving, supplying, providing God for your life. We talk about wanting to be like God and wanting to take on the characteristics of God, but often fail to imitate God. We're never more like God than when we give. An attitude of giving is an attitude of confidence that says "God is my source; I can give because I serve El-Shaddai, the giving God!"

Imagine standing at a waterfall and watching the continuous, unending flow of water going over the edge. We have a great waterfall not far from where I live called Snoqualmie Falls. I first went to the waterfall in 1982. Since then I've gone back many times. The amazing thing is that the water is still continuing to cascade over the edge, night and day, twenty-four hours a day, year after year it just keeps on flowing. Now, imagine wanting to take in as much as you can of the water. How can you receive it? The first thing that comes to mind is a container. So what size is the container of choice? Is it teacup size? Water bottle size? Barrel size? Only the size of your container can limit the amount of water you can capture at the great waterfall. The question is not one of supply but of ability to contain. It is the same with God's supply for our lives. He wants us to be free from limited thinking that causes us to be reluctant givers. He wants us to see Him like the unending waterfall, providing a constant supply of more than enough.

When we see God's provision this way, we automatically think generously about giving. We believe *there is more where it came from*, therefore it is not hard to give it up. This attitude of generous, liberal giving then results in an increasing capacity to receive.

"IN LIFE, AS IN
FOOTBALL, YOU WON'T
GO FAR UNLESS YOU
KNOW WHERE THE GOAL
POSTS ARE."
—ARNOLD GLASOU

Chapter 9

OPPOSING POVERTY PROVERB #4

**Opposing Poverty Proverb #4
Have a plan for profit.**

"The plans of the diligent lead to profit..."
Proverbs 21:5 (NIV)

In the 1950's, a study was done at Harvard University on goal setting and planning. The graduating class of 1953 was interviewed and each person was asked if they had specific goals and a plan to achieve them.

Only three percent had clear goals and a plan to accomplish them. Twenty years later, in 1973, researchers located the members of the class of 1953. They discovered that the three percent with a plan for their future were worth more financially than the other 97 percent combined! They also seemed to be happier and healthier than those who had graduated college without a plan for their future.

When some Christians are asked what their plans are for the future, they respond with spiritual sounding dialogue like, "I'm just trusting the Lord" or "I'll do whatever God wants me to do." The fact is they don't have a plan, and these *pat* spiritual sounding cliches serve to shift the responsibility of their future over to God. Successful planning for your future takes thought, time, prayer, research, and meditation. Most people spend more time planning a holiday than they do planning their future.

God Is A Planner
The manner with which God brings forth the future is not by impulse or reaction, but by planning.

"But the plans of the Lord stand firm forever, the purposes of His heart through all generations."
Psalm 33:11 (NIV)

*"For I know the plans I have for you,' declares the
Lord. 'Plans to prosper you and not harm
you, plans to give you a hope and a future."
Jeremiah 29:11 (NIV)*

Notice in this scripture, God's plan is prosperity. His
plan for the future is definitive and it's good. For
those of us who want to be like God, this is an
important attribute of His nature that we can apply
to our lives...PLAN FOR A PROSPEROUS, HOPE-
FILLED FUTURE!

When we moved from one house to another, we lost
track of our remote control. Like most men, I felt I
had lost control of my life without a remote in my
hand. We purchased a new remote, brought it home
and started pushing buttons but nothing happened.
That's when I realized that I had to take the time to
synchronize my new remote with the TV set before it
could fulfill its purpose. In a similar way, we are all
created with a purpose. There is a functional role for
which God equipped us. Each of us will remain
unfulfilled until we are active in our purpose.
However, we have to take the time to locate God's
plan for us and synchronize our lives to it. Since we
know His plan is to "prosper us... not to harm us, to
give us a hope and a future," we have to tune into
and plan for it in order to be synchronized with His
plan for our lives.

When you take the time to synchronize your plans with God's plan, you will find yourself functioning in an area you are qualified to function in and being fulfilled doing so. Remember, "haste leads to poverty" whether it's planning your career or your retirement. Take time to plan with diligence — it leads to profit.

One of the most fascinating books I have ever read is the life story of Monty Roberts. The book is entitled *The Man Who Listens To Horses.* In the book he tells about his early days as a rodeo rider and his problems with his violent, horse-trainer father. Refusing to accept the abusive conventional method of horse training, Monty has spent his whole life working with horses, schooling them, listening to them, and learning their ancient equine language. He can take a wild, high strung horse that has never before been handled and persuade that horse to accept a bit, a bridle, a saddle, and rider in thirty minutes. The Queen of England, after hearing about his method of horse training, invited him to demonstrate his technique at Windsor Castle in 1989. Now, all the Queen's horses are trained Monty's way. He is now a legend as a real-life "horse whisperer", highly respected for his undeniable success. In his last year of high school, Monty was given the assignment of articulating his plans for the future. The teacher, Mr. Fowler, also insisted "this vision must be realistic." Monty felt ready for this assignment, since he had known what he wanted to do in life from the time he was nine-years old. His dream had been so clear in his mind that he had been sketching stables and training facilities. When Monty turned in what he thought was a good paper, it was returned to him with a big red "F" printed at the top of the page. Monty met with Mr. Fowler and asked him what he had done wrong. "Do you realize that the average annual income of a person in the United States is $6,300? What makes you think you can afford this?", Mr. Fowler asked. "I know your family and background. It would just not be possible. Take this paper home, think about it and change your vision to make it realistic." Although Monty was surprised and shaken by the incident, after discussing it with his mom, he returned it to Mr. Fowler as it was, without changes. He also attached a note to Mr. Fowler suggesting that while he could grade the paper as he saw fit, perhaps he did not have the right to put a cap on anyone's aspirations. Years later, the same Mr. Fowler led a group of senior citizens on a tour of Monty's "Flag is up Farms." At the end of the tour, with Monty at his side, he told everyone, "A teacher doesn't have a right to put a cap on the aspirations of his students. Today we are looking at what I thought was an unattainable goal for Monty's life."

Never allow a lack of resources to stop you from setting goals and planning your future. What is realistic tomorrow is not determined by what is in your bank account today. A lack of finances should never keep you from planning for a prosperous future. A lot of people wait for the provision to come before they start to plan. What these people do not realize is that the provision is awaiting a worthwhile plan.

A personal example of this is an experience I had several years ago as I stepped off a plane in Wisconsin. I knew I had one of my most challenging days ahead of me. In the hours that followed, it was my intention to convince the board members of the largest church bonds company in America that I could assume responsibility for a 4.5 million dollar loan that was in default.

The one thing I had going for me that day, as I faced six men I had never met before, was a God-given plan of prosperity. Anyone who has dealt with bankers knows that it is their job to tell you why something won't work. This plan, however, found favor with those sophisticated, financial minds. After a full day of questions and answers, we were on our way to assuming responsibility for a debt of nearly five million dollars. Why would I want the debt, you ask? Because the appraised property value was twelve to fourteen million dollars. The interesting element, however, was that we did not have the finances to pay for the debt. What we had was a God-given, specific plan for prosperity. Part of the plan called for us to refinance the entire loan within one year. This seemed impossible because of its history as a troubled loan and our unproven ability. In fact, the bond company agreed that if we succeeded in refinancing, they would deduct $250,000 off the note. All of this was in the written plan, and in less than one year the miracle provision had come. We were refinanced with a brand new lender. As of this writing, that has been six plus years and the plans to prosper continue in our ministry.

What I am saying is don't plan small. Don't think in terms of barely getting by. Don't allow your current ability to hinder you from planning BIG for your future. When you plan for profit and plan for prosperity, you oppose the limiting, restricting force of poverty in your life.

"THERE IS ENOUGH IN THE WORLD FOR EVERYONE TO HAVE PLENTY TO LIVE ON HAPPILY AND TO BE AT PEACE WITH HIS NEIGHBORS."
—HARRY S. TRUMAN

Chapter 10

Opposing Poverty Proverb #5

"The rich rule over the poor, and the borrower
is servant to the lender."
Proverbs 22:7 (NIV)

This may surprise you, but I don't believe the Bible
is opposed to *debt*. I do believe the Bible is opposed

to *excessive* debt. The danger of borrowing can vary depending on whom you borrow from and how much you borrow. In civilized, institutionalized America, borrowing has become much more user-friendly. In Bible times, if you had a debt you could not pay, the creditor had a legal right to take your children into slavery (Leviticus 25). God showed a great deal of compassion for people who were "debt slaves" and "debt prisoners" in the Old Testament. That's why He called for a year of *Jubilee*. Jubilee was a year where land lost by excessive debt would be returned to the original owner. Children in slavery, (paying back a creditor's debt) would be free to go back to their home. Jesus said (Luke 4:18-19) "I have come to proclaim the year of Jubilee... setting free of those in (debtors') prison." Today there is more compassion for those in society who are in debt. America's economy is strong because of our free-market economy with debt. If borrowing and lending stopped in America, our economy would collapse. Our standard of living is high because there is plenty of money to borrow and lend. If borrowing were completely wrong then lending would have to be wrong also. But, in certain circumstances, the Bible encourages lending.

"Rather be openhanded and freely lend
him whatever he needs."
Deuteronomy 15:8 (NIV)

*"They are always generous and lend freely; their
children will be blessed."*
Psalm 37:26 (NIV)

Nehemiah jump started the economy by encouraging
lending to those in need.

*"I and my brothers and my men are also lending the
people money and grain. But let the
exacting of usury stop!"*
Nehemiah 5:10 (NIV)

*The key to borrowing is that you do it strategically and
not excessively.* About five years into our marriage,
Sheila and I found ourselves in excessive credit card
debt. Like many couples, we had good intentions but
were misled by the easy purchase power of credit
cards. After committing our situation to God, we
stopped using credit cards completely. God helped
us, and we applied ourselves to learn new use of credit
rules. Only in recent years have we allowed ourselves
the convenience of a credit card. Some who read this
book need to do what we did. You need to cut the
plastic until you can control it.

SOME BIBLE TEACHERS PROMOTE THE IDEA THAT CHRISTIANS SHOULD HAVE NO DEBT.

The scripture this teaching originates from is Romans

13:8 which reads:

"Let no debt remain outstanding, except the continuing debt to love one another, for he who loves his fellowman has fulfilled the law."
Romans 13:8 (NIV)

Although throughout the Bible we are cautioned to avoid excessive debt, we are never taught that we should have no debt. The above scripture is teaching us that we should pay what is due or "outstanding" debt. *The intent of the writer was to tell Christians to pay their bills on time, whether it was a house payment, taxes, or money borrowed from a friend.* Technically, in fact, we all borrow something. For example, your utility company bills you for usage of gas, electricity, and telephones every month. The time between your usage and your payment is a "loan" to you based on their confidence that you will pay. What I'm saying is that borrowing from a lender when it is within your ability to repay may prove beneficial for you as well as the lender. Perhaps you are wondering why I would write about this when there are undeniable dangers of debt referenced repeatedly in scripture. The reason is that if a person doesn't understand *exactly* what scripture says about debt, they can, in some situations, hurt themselves by refusing to get a loan that they can afford. For example, people who wait until they can pay cash for a home will *lose* money by paying rent over an extended time and may never be able to afford adequate housing because of the rate of inflation. In other words, by the time they can afford the $120,000 house, it will be a $150,000 house! Churches and businesses who need to build facilities to accommodate growth, can stagnate and die if they are unwilling to borrow.

In situations like these, a borrower can actually benefit financially from a loan. Did you know that corporate America borrows even when it doesn't have to because it makes financial sense? The company you work for probably uses debt as leverage. Through the sales of stock, bonds, and creative financing most companies remain strong in the marketplace. Let's review some of the basics of Bible economics related to borrowing and lending.

BORROWING AND LENDING BY THE BIBLE

1. If borrowing was forbidden by scripture, we would not be encouraged to lend. Here are two examples of borrowing and lending without a negative connotation:

"If a man borrows an animal from his neighbor and it is injured or dies while the owner is not present, he must make restitution."
Exodus 22:14 (NIV)

2. The borrower is "obligated" to the lender.

> *"The rich ruleth over the poor, and the*
> *borrower is servant to the lender."*
> *Proverbs 22:7 (KJV)*

3. As Christians we should never practice usury when we are helping another Christian get through a difficult circumstance.

> *"If thou lend money to any of my people that is poor by*
> *thee, thou shalt not be to him as a usurer, neither shalt*
> *thou lay upon him usury."*
> *Exodus 22:25 (KJV)*

The modern translations of scripture often translate "usury" into "interest." Usury, however, is defined in the dictionary as an *exorbitant* rate of interest. Often people in a financial crisis are taken advantage of by lenders who practice usury.

4. Avoid excessive borrowing since too much debt can cause financial hardship.

5. Don't mortgage your home or business to provide a crisis loan to a friend.

"My son, if you have put up security for your neighbor, if you have struck hands in pledge for another, if you have been trapped by what you said, ensnared by the words of your mouth, then do this, my son, to free yourself, since you have fallen into your neighbor's hands: Go and humble yourself: press your plea with your neighbor! Allow no sleep to your eyes, no slumber to your eyelids. Free yourself, like a gazelle from the hand of the hunter, like a bird from the snare of the fowler."
Proverbs 6:1-5 (NIV)

"He who puts up security for another will surely suffer, but whoever refuses to strike hands in pledge is safe."
Proverbs 11:15 (NIV)

"Give a man a fish, feed him for a day. Teach him how to fish, feed him for a lifetime."
—Anonymous

Chapter 11

Opposing Poverty Proverb #6

> ## Opposing Poverty Proverb #6
> ## Be wise in your approach to helping
> ## others who are in need.

*"A man lacking in judgment strikes hands in a pledge
and puts up security for his neighbor."*
Proverbs 17:18 (NIV)

Part of being a Christian is to want to help people in
need. Sometimes this compulsion causes a Christian

to violate wisdom principles for their own lives. One of the basic guidelines for helping rescue a person in trouble, is for the rescuer to stay in a secure place themselves. For example, if you are in a boat and you are trying to save someone who is drowning, your first choice of rescue is to throw them a lifeline. If you leave the safety of the boat, you can lessen your chances of a successful rescue. By leaving the boat, not only does the drowning person have no link to the safety of the boat, but you have now put yourself at risk. The same is true when someone is in trouble financially. Don't forfeit your position of strength and safety by putting your home or savings up as collateral.

I have watched well-meaning, big hearted people give their savings to a Christian friend who was in trouble. Before doing this a person should consider the fact that the savings is not only theirs but their spouse's and children's. In other words, don't risk losing your children's inheritance without careful consideration of your responsibility to them. Your family's security is your first responsibility. I do believe in helping people, but the proverbs send us a message that we should help while remaining in a position of strength ourselves. Forfeiting your strength by putting up security is not the proper way to help someone else.

When you have an opportunity to help someone and it doesn't mean forfeiting your position of financial strength, by all means be willing to help.

The reason I emphasize being willing is because I do believe there are times when the worst thing we can do for someone is to continue to bail them out of trouble.

> *"A hot-tempered man must pay the penalty; if you rescue him, you will have to do it again."*
> *Proverbs 19:19 (NIV)*

Some occasions call for us to give to someone in need, while in other circumstances, charity has become a source of enabling people to continue wrong behavior. It's not always easy to know if we should or should not help financially. After doing your best to discern the situation (the person's lifestyle habits and their level of integrity) helping may be the right thing to do. When you do it, do it as unto the Lord.

> *"He who has pity on the poor lends to the Lord, and that which he has given He will repay to him."*
> *Proverbs 19:17 (AMP)*

CHARITY AT ITS WORST
The welfare programs in the U.S. have not worked. Rather than helping eliminate poverty, the welfare

efforts which began in 1964 actually increased social welfare spending more than twenty times in twenty years! The amount of people who were poor and dependent increased rather than decreased. After billions of dollars have been spent, poverty has grown in America. WHY? Because the war on poverty cannot be won by giving someone a blanket and providing them a meal. Homeless people are at best "sustained" when given a place to sleep. The approach of temporary relief without providing long-term solutions is charity at its worst. When we provide only temporary relief from the threat of poverty, not only will we need to do it for the same people tomorrow, but we also make it easier for others to become dependent on that same temporary relief. By feeding and clothing the poor without requiring and empowering them to work, we rob them of their dignity. I'm not advocating that we stop meeting the basic needs of the poor, but that we recognize the need to assist people in a transition from welfare to work. Anything less than this is *charity*, but it is charity at its *worst*. The church must lead the way in guiding people out of a poverty mentality and into a productive life. This will not happen simply by having compassion on those in need. We must take on the larger task of equipping people with knowledge and dignity.

Over the past several years, our church has been involved in various ways of helping the needy in our community. We have a great team of volunteers who spend countless hours in Operation Care, our food distribution program. Currently, approximately fifteen hundred people per month receive three to five days (three meals per day) of food. We distribute approximately forty thousand pounds of food per month. Although we have viewed this effort as an important display of love and compassion, we have concluded that it is incomplete.

An Improved Approach To Charity

Our introduction to Wings came when my wife Sheila met Wings founder, Kevin Bradley, at a seminar in Dallas. Kevin, who is a former stock broker for Legg Mason in Baltimore, has designed a forty-hour life skills training course which teaches someone to make the transition from welfare to work. Wings has an 82% success rate (and growing) in moving people off welfare. This program has been the topic of discussion in the House Budget Committee in Washington, D.C. and commissioned by House Speaker, Newt Gingrich, to be taken nationally as a model solution for welfare reform. Some statistics of the Wings program are listed below:

- 75% of Wings graduates are employed within the first week of graduation.

- The average wage of a Wings graduate is $7.80 an hour.
- The retention level of employment is 90% after six months of graduation.
- Wings is 100% privately funded and costs the tax payers *nothing*.
- For a class of twenty Wings students, the cost per student is approximately $350 while similar programs conducted by the government cost over $3,500 per student.
- It is estimated that Wings will save taxpayers over six million dollars in social welfare cost this year.

There was an additional point of information I found interesting in Kevin Bradley's research. In the church studies he conducted of ministries helping the needy, 97% went to RELIEF while only 3% was going to a development program. I know we fell into that category until we were introduced to Wings. Now, we are looking forward to a wiser approach in helping those in need. Thanks to Kevin Bradley and others who are involved in an intelligent war on poverty.

With "Gleaning" As Our Guide
One of the creative ways that God instructed Israel to help the poor was in something the Bible refers to as "gleaning" (Leviticus 19:9; 19:10; 23:22 and Deuteronomy 24:19-21). In this planned approach of assistance to those in need, a farmer was prohibited

from completely harvesting his field of crops. The poor were then allowed to glean whatever harvest was there. There are three considerations about gleaning that can help guide us in our obligation to the poor.

First, the farmer was not expected to give the poor what he needed for his family and the marketplace. He was expected to harvest almost all of his field, leaving "the very edges" and to "not pick up what may have fallen to the ground." Again, it is essential that those who can operate from a place of strength not forfeit that position, because of a desire to give to the poor. When giving to the poor, don't give in excess of what you can afford to give. Think like a farmer who must retain strength to buy more land and produce more crops.

Secondly, it appears that landowners had the right to specify who could glean from their land (Ruth 2). I think all efforts to help the poor should be concerned with individuals and not just the community of those in need. We can practice this principle by supporting organizations who are selective in their approach. Occasionally, I have given to people on the streets, but I give the majority of my donations to the needy through organizations who are focusing on helping families and children. To me, the administrative cost of the organization is well worth the benefit of a selective, targeted approached.

Thirdly, gleaning was hard work. The crops and the fruit were not gathered on behalf of the poor. God did not ask the community to prepare the food and deliver it to the poor. He simply asked them to do their part in making it available and accessible. By using this approach, the poor and hungry were not exempt from the work ethic. If they wanted to eat, they had to be willing to work. The Apostle Paul verified this as a beneficial principle in society when he said, "If a man will not work, he shall not eat." (II Thessalonians 3:10)

Through these three characteristics of gleaning, it is safe to conclude that God had a definite reason for this approach. Likewise, how we as individuals approach our giving to those in need should not be strictly based on compassion. Many people have an unconscious compassion for help the needy. These people who resist logic and principle, often find themselves engulfed in their own lack and insufficiency. This eventually creates a community of people who cannot help themselves, much less help one another. This is all the more reason to be wise in our approach to helping others who are in need.

"'To get, we must give; to accumulate, we must scatter; to make ourselves happy, we must make others happy.'
—C.H. Spurgeon

Chapter 12

OPPOSING POVERTY PROVERB #7

Opposing Poverty Proverb #7
Seek the success of those you serve

"He who tends a fig tree will eat its fruit, and he who looks after his master will be honored."
Proverbs 27:18 (NIV)

All of us must recognize and take care of the fig trees in our lives. Depending on your specific position, the fig tree may be a customer, a project, a company, an employer, a pastor, a secretary, or an administrator.

In the mid-1960's, Lee Iacocca was a Vice President for the Ford Motor Company. In an effort to improve his division's sales performance, he did massive research on the people who ultimately determine the success of a company — the consumers. His research pointed him to a specific and widespread interest for a sporty car with a lot of style and a low price tag. Equipped with a clear understanding of how he could serve people's interest, Iacocca led the creation of Ford's now famous Mustang. The Mustang became the car of the sixties and led directly to Iacocca's fame in the auto industry.

In the mid 1970's, a young pastor named Bill Hybels conducted a survey in a suburb of Chicago to identify how he could serve the spiritual needs of the people. He now credits the growth of America's largest congregation to the "seeker-sensitive" approach. While others were standing around asking why more people weren't going to church, Bill took the time and gave an enormous amount of energy to develop a church that would be focused on meeting the needs of people. Willow Creek Community Church has become a model to various church organizations on the importance of becoming a servant to the modern day needs of people. More churches are discovering how to seek the success of those they serve. This is quite a paradigm shift from the previous approach to ministry, which showed little interest in helping people succeed. Today, many churches are providing relevant church services and practical Bible teachings that equip and minister to those who attend.

Whether you're building automobiles or building lives, the principle is the same: A person cannot succeed in life unless they find a way to serve the interests and needs of others.

SERVING AT WORK

> *"Slaves, obey your earthly masters with respect and fear, and with sincerity of heart, just as you would obey Christ. Obey them not only to win their favor when their eye is on you, but like slaves of Christ, doing the will of God from your heart. Serve wholeheartedly, as if you were serving the Lord, not men." Ephesians 6:5-7 (NIV)*

The word "slave" here is equivalent to the term "employee" in today's marketplace. As an employee, seeking the success of those you serve will move you into an elite, sought-after group of individuals whose employers literally trust you with their lives. When you seek the success of those you serve, you move beyond the thought of "just doing your job", and take on a genuine interest in the success of your company. I've always had a special interest in entrepreneurs and business owners. Having had the opportunity to know many and discuss their businesses with them, it's amazing how they echo the same cliche, "It's hard to find good help." What these business owners are actually saying is that "few people take a genuine interest in my company's success." If you want to create job security where you are, or if you hope to someday have your own business, go to work everyday with the goal of making the people you work for successful. The above scripture emphasizes a specific approach to work that is repeated several times in scripture.

"Whatever you do, work at it with all your heart as working for the Lord and not men."
Colossians 3:23 (NIV)

Some people read this and misunderstand its message. This is not intended to take honor away from an employer but rather to increase it. The instruction, if followed, will result in the utmost respect and wholehearted effort on the part of an employee.

NEGLECTING THE GOOSE

Remember the fable of the goose and the golden egg?

This fable is about a poor farmer whose pet goose produces a glittering golden egg. The farmer can't believe what's happening to him when the same thing occurs again the next day. Unfortunately, with his increasing wealth, he becomes greedy and impatient. He decides to kill the goose and get all of the eggs at once. But when he opens the goose, he finds it empty. There are no golden eggs and now he has eliminated the means of production. Most people consider themselves wiser than the foolish farmer. The fact is, however, that many people are *neglecting* the goose of productivity in their life.

- When a waitress doesn't care if the customer is enjoying dining at the restaurant, the waitress is "neglecting the goose."
- When a receptionist is impatient and rude to a caller, the receptionist is "neglecting the goose."
- When a company has no quality controls, the management is "neglecting the goose."
- When a church fails to invest in the tools of ministry and the place of worship, its leadership is "neglecting the goose."
- When lower management fails to support and strengthen upper management, they "neglect the goose."
- When companies do not invest in the ongoing training of their management, they "neglect the goose."

- When a church doesn't take good care of the pastors, they are "neglecting the goose".

In 1946, the Hewlett Packard company was less than ten years old when their revenue was cut by fifty percent. The cut came because they were a large supplier to the United States government in World War II, and when the war ended, so did many of their contracts. The amazing response they took was not to retreat but to advance. They did so by taking advantage of the fact that many companies in similar situations were releasing some of their best employees. Hewlett Packard actually hired some talented scientists and engineers during one of its most difficult times. The investment in the company paid off big over the next two decades as the engineering team introduced many new and innovative products which brought prosperity to Hewlett Packard. In this powerful and courageous endeavor, the company recommitted itself to locating new needs in society and the employees committed themselves to the goals of the company.

I remember, during a challenging financial endeavor in our ministry, being asked by a mission-minded church member, "Will we continue to give to missions?" I responded by saying, "Absolutely...but we must also invest in our ministry here at home, so we can continue to give more to missions for many years to come."

IDENTIFYING THE GOOSE AND KEEPING IT HEALTHY

The goose could be a top notch worker, a customer, the people who gave you your job, or the people who attend your church. But, *seek the success of those you serve* and poverty will have one less point of entry in your life. Seeking the success of those you serve should not be mistaken as submitting yourself to careless disregard for your best interests. The ability to recognize those who *add* to our lives and look after their best interests is not only noble but also wise. When Jesus told His disciples "the greatest among you will be your servant", He was *not* simply saying "go find a servant robe and you will be great." But, He was addressing the principle issue of *how to be great*. This teaching has been proven time and again throughout history. Those whom we recognize as truly great are those who have given themselves in servant-like fashion to face the greatest challenges of life. If you're looking for great people, you will find them taking on problems that ordinary men avoid. Great people take on Goliath-sized problems while others only discuss their dilemma. In every profitable organization there is a servant mind-set. The servant may be dressed like a king and eat daily at a banquet table, but business doesn't succeed without a servant's commitment.

When you are in the presence of people who have grown an institution, business, ministry, or city into a place of strength and prosperity, you are in the presence of someone who knows how to serve. These people are usually more applauded by their peers, than by others. The reason for this is their peers recognize the tremendous servant-like dedication essential to their accomplishments.

Erik Van Alstine is a lay pastor in our church. When he and his wife Sandy began their company, there were no employees and no cash flow. Together, they committed themselves to starting a business by serving the communication needs of small organizations. They faced the challenges of producing quality communication materials for business owners who themselves either could not or did not, want the added headache to produce these materials. When you seek the interests of those you serve, they value your work. Business grew for Erik and Sandy. After seven years, their company sales are expected to reach five million dollars this year. Today the company, Signature Media Services, in Tacoma, Washington, has other highly qualified managers and partners in the company. Sandy is busy being a mom to their five children, but the servant dedication is still there. All the new, bright, talented people who have found an enjoyable place to work may think that it all came easily or could underestimate the value of the entrepreneurial spirit that birthed the company they work for. Those who don't take it for granted will do for their company exactly what Erik and Sandy did when they started — they will seek the success of those they serve. This principle is one of the most powerful oppositions of poverty available to all of us. Look around you, locate the fig tree, identify the goose. They are there in your world, camouflaged as managers, customers, and organizations. Once you locate them, seek their success and serve them well.

"BUT REMEMBER THE
LORD YOUR GOD,
FOR IT IS HE WHO GIVES
YOU THE ABILITY TO
PRODUCE WEALTH THAT
HE MAY
ESTABLISH HIS
COVENANT."
DEUTERONOMY 8:18

Chapter 13

THE POWER TO GET WEALTH

THE POWER TO GET WEALTH

In the Northwest, it's common sport to go fishing off the coast. Many times I have watched seagulls follow fishing boats into shore. These birds expect a free lunch provided as fishermen clean their fish and put the leftovers in the water. In Monterey, California, this same scene had occurred for years. Fishermen would throw the fish entrails to the pelicans day after day. There was a dramatic change, however, when a new commercial market was found for the entrails. The pelicans no longer had a free meal, yet they made no effort to fish for themselves. Assuming they were powerless, many starved to death. It was an interesting circumstance to observe and was newsworthy enough to receive media attention. Although these pelicans had a God-given ability to fish, they were totally blind to their own ability. Is it possible that I am blind to my own power to get wealth? The question is, "Do I have greater wealth-getting power than I am presently using?"

USING YOUR RESOURCES

We all have resources even in times of shortage. The famous Colonel Sanders, creator of the recipe for Kentucky Fried Chicken, is an example of this. At the age of sixty-one he took his recipe on the road. After more than one thousand rejections, he found someone who was willing to pay him for the right to sell his recipe in a national franchise. In all of us there is a God-given power to get wealth. It may be agriculture, farming, selling, producing, building, or it may be as an artist or musician, but there is definitely a power within you. The power to lead, speak, negotiate, manage, solve problems or administrate may be within you and you're not even aware of it. A painter gets paid for painting and a gardener gets paid for gardening. There is a direct correlation between what you do, the service you provide, and its financial value. In almost every occupation, there are people with a reputation for excellence. These people are compensated at higher levels in their particular occupation than others. The reason is that there are people who are either willing to pay them more, or there are more people willing to pay them. The power to get wealth, much like the power of electricity, must be harnessed and utilized to get maximum results. The choices each individual makes about what we *do* is our way of tapping into a God-given power to get wealth. Choices of education, investment, and careers are all directly related to our own individual power usage. The power to get wealth is a power available to all of us. The degree that we tap into it is related to our choices. I am not suggesting that you should make all of your choices based on how much money is in it, but I am saying that wealth and prosperity is important to you and it should be! Make some choices that will lead to prosperity.

OVERCOMING ADVERSITY
After his parents were brutally murdered in North Vietnam, Ri moved to South Vietnam. While there, Ri went to school and eventually became a building contractor. He prospered greatly until he was arrested on a trip north. After being imprisoned in North Vietnam for three years, he finally escaped to South Vietnam. When he learned that the U.S. was pulling out of South Vietnam, he gave all his worldly possessions in exchange for passage on a small, overcrowded fishing boat. He was later picked up on

the high seas by an American ship and taken to the Philippines. Once there, he lived in a refugee camp for two years, until he was allowed to come to the United States. When he arrived in the U.S., Ri's cousin offered both him and his wife jobs in his tailor shop. Even though their net pay was only $300 per week, they were determined to succeed. For two years they lived in the back room of the tailor shop and took sponge baths so they could save every penny possible. Within two years they had saved $30,000 and bought out the cousin's business. It was only then that Ri rented an apartment. Today Ri is a millionaire.

This modern day story of success reminds me of the life of Joseph in the book of Genesis. Joseph faced adversity and continued to prosper. Although he began as a slave in a country where no one knew him, God's favor was upon him.

"The Lord was with Joseph and he prospered, and he lived in the house of his Egyptian master. When his master saw that the Lord was with him and that the Lord gave him success in everything he did,..."
Genesis 39: 2, 3 (NIV)

Joseph's power to get wealth could not be stopped by those who lied about him or those who mistreated him. He went from the prison to the palace. He went from poverty to a place of prosperity. Pharaoh gave him access to all the wealth of the most powerful nation in the world at that time. Joseph's rise to a position of power placed him in charge of vast resources.

Never allow adversity to convince you that you are powerless. Perhaps you are in a season of setbacks in your life. Don't interpret the setback to be permanent. There is a power within you.

The greatest waste of a person's potential is in the survival mode. The power to get wealth is untapped and dormant when the goal is to simply "get by." Several years ago an archeologist discovered seeds in an Egyptian pyramid that had been preserved in an airtight encasing. Although the seeds were estimated to be two thousand years old, when scientists planted some of the seeds, they still brought forth life. The purpose and potential of the seeds was locked deep within them and remained dormant all those years. In a similar way, many people exist in a survival mode while their purpose is unfulfilled.

"The purposes of a man's heart are deep waters, but a man of understanding draws them out."
Proverbs 20:5 (NIV)

Remember this, our power to get wealth is attached

to our purpose. When the two are not connected in some significant way, the result is a survival way of life. People of purpose have a certainty about life, a confidence that moves them forward. People without purpose, on the other hand, are always uncertain, unsure, and in pursuit of nothing. To help you with the discovery of your purpose, realize that your purpose is already within you. It may be "deep waters," but with understanding you can "draw it out." By unlocking the depths of your most individual and natural attributes, you can begin to discover your purpose. Your purpose should not be confused with your goals. Purpose cannot be reached and checked off like goals can. Neither should purpose be mistaken as what your parents expected from you. Purpose is not discovered by asking "what would I like to be?". People who assume that find themselves chasing fantasies and wish lists. This is as unfruitful as an oak tree attempting to grow oranges. Can the mighty oak be productive? Absolutely! Can the mighty oak be strong and healthy? Definitely! But the oak tree is not created to produce oranges, bananas or strawberries. Its purpose is acorns. Another important thing to know is that your purpose is not your career. It supersedes your career. For example, a person's purpose could be to "solve difficult problems and provide meaningful solutions." A variety of careers that would work comfortably within this purpose would be:

- Dentist
- Accountant
- Mechanic
- Architect
- Counselor
- Computer Programmer

So, don't make the mistake of thinking your career is your purpose. If you locate your purpose, it will supersede any specific career option. So, how is your purpose attached to your power to get wealth? Simply by focusing daily on incorporating your purpose into everything you do. Not incorporating your purpose into your life, career and future is like a recipe missing a key ingredient. For example, I know that my purpose is "to locate and communicate wisdom." That has become my primary focus in ministry. There are many valid forms of ministry that I could attempt to excel in and would find myself drained, exhausted, and unfulfilled. By incorporating and focusing on the locating and communication of wisdom, I fulfill my purpose and remain productive. However, the great discovery is that my purpose is not limited to ministry. If I apply my purpose to my parenting, I enjoy and am fulfilled as a father. If I apply my purpose to my personal life, I bring a contribution to my family, friends, and peers. It's when I'm in this flow that I sense God has equipped me for a worthwhile and rewarding service to those around me. The result is the opportunity to serve on various ministry boards, write books, minister in many churches, and participate in some unique challenges.

Envision life like a potluck dinner and ask yourself "what do I bring to the table?". What is my greatest contribution to those around me that I can provide continually because it's within me? Now, bring that every day in a spirit of excellence to your world and watch the favor of God and man rest upon you. This constant release of purpose in your life will result in an increase of opportunity. People will appreciate and reward you for the contribution you make. Don't do it to "get," but watch what happens when your God-given power to get wealth is released from within you. When living in your purpose, resources that otherwise would be scarce, become plentiful. Ephesians 2:10 verifies that "we are God's workmanship, created in Christ Jesus to do good works, which God prepared in advance for us to do." Notice we are already created with specific accomplishments in mind. Energy used in other ways can never be as fulfilling as energy used to accomplish what God prepared in advance for us to do.

In conclusion, this book is less about the pursuit of wealth than it is the pursuit of purpose. The conviction with which I've written this book is that prosperity, fruitfulness, and abundance are a direct result of our discovery of our Creator's intentions for our life.

Would you like more wisdom for your life? The following products are available for you today!

BOOKS

RAISING CHAMPION CHILDREN $6.00
We all want our children to have success in life. As parents, what we invest in our children now is the determining factor as to what they become in the future. This book discusses the essential ingredients you'll need in raising your children to be champions.

THE PROVING GROUND $9.95
Every believer faces several "tests" in their life. Testing always precedes promotion. Divine promotion only comes through the "proving" of one's personal potential. This book instructs the reader in the correct attitudes and behavior they'll need to "pass the test" in life.

CHARACTERISTICS OF A WINNER $8.00
God has destined each and every one of us to be winners! He shows us that it takes specific attributes to excel in life. This book teaches seven characteristics of a winner, in a practical and easy to understand manner. *Characteristics of a Winner* offers us several living examples from God's Word on how to win in life.

DEVELOPING CONFIDENCE   **$5.00**

Confidence is something that everyone needs. Unfortunately, many believers today although they have great confidence in God's power, have little or no confidence in themselves and their own abilities. This book has been written to identify those things that can undermine your confidence, as well as to teach principles for building healthy, godly self confidence in your life.

HABITS *(OVERCOMING NEGATIVE BEHAVIOR)*   **$3.50**

A habit is a pattern of behavior. Although often seen as negative, habits can be extremely positive. This book will provide insight on how to use the power of habits to your advantage and become the person that God intended you to be.

To order your "Wisdom for Life" product, please mail your check to:

**Kevin Gerald Communications
1819 E. 72nd St.
Tacoma, WA 98404**

For more information or to charge by phone, call:
(253) 475-6454

Please add $1.50 for shipping and handling to each book you order.